Onkere

To Ben, from the author.

Pr. Blanchard ONANGA.

Onkere

An African Boy's Story of
Struggle, Resilience, and Determination

DR. BLANCHARD ONANGA NDJILA

ONKERE
AN AFRICAN BOY'S STORY OF STRUGGLE, RESILIENCE, AND DETERMINATION

iUniverse books may be ordered through booksellers or by contacting:

iUniverse
1663 Liberty Drive
Bloomington, IN 47403
www.iuniverse.com
1-800-Authors (1-800-288-4677)

Because of the dynamic nature of the Internet, any web addresses or links contained in this book may have changed since publication and may no longer be valid. The views expressed in this work are solely those of the author and do not necessarily reflect the views of the publisher, and the publisher hereby disclaims any responsibility for them.

The views expressed in this work are solely those of the author and do not necessarily reflect the views of the publisher, and the publisher hereby disclaims any responsibility for them.

Any people depicted in stock imagery provided by Getty Images are models, and such images are being used for illustrative purposes only. Certain stock imagery © Getty Images.

ISBN: 978-1-5320-7605-3 (sc)
ISBN: 978-1-5320-7606-0 (e)

Library of Congress Control Number: 2019942721

Print information available on the last page.

iUniverse rev. date: 05/29/2019

To all the people who helped me become the person I am: my parents, Raymond and Regina Onanga; my children, Aubree, Owen, Sylvie, and Ameliah Onanga; my brothers and sisters; my nieces and nephews; my cousins; my friends; my in-laws; and my wife, Kiersten Klink Onanga.

Introduction

The story you are about to read is based on a true story that the narrator felt needed to be publicly shared, given the fact that time, as is well known, has the capacity to weaken and affect humans' ability to remember past events that occurred a decade or score years ago. Keeping this sober reality in mind, I felt compelled to jot down this story on paper. Personal pronouns "I" and "he" will be used interchangeably, though from different points of view to refer to Onkere, the main character of the story being narrated. The personal pronoun "I" will be specifically used when the narrator implicates himself and narrates from his point of view the events being described, whereas whenever he detaches Onkere from the narration, he will specifically use the personal pronoun "he" or "Onkere." Additionally, personal pronoun "we" will be used to imply the narrator is in a group event. The main objective of using this alternating narrative technique is to keep readers awake so that they pay attention to the evolvement of the story. It is also used to allow them to further explore the story in such a way that they know who is doing what, as well as when and why. The story being narrated is the author's. Therefore, the main protagonist is simply his surrogate. As for the story, it basically deals with how a young, enthusiastically determined, highly spirited, and intellectually motivated boy named Onkere, from Mpugu, a French-speaking country located in West Africa, came to passionately fall in love with both the English language and American culture. In other words, the story highlights how he intensely came to discover the Anglo-Saxon world.

More specifically, it discusses the people who most likely influenced his learning of English and, on the other hand, those who helped him along the way go to places he went to in order to improve his skills of the language. I will also be addressing some of the strategies he used to improve his understanding and way of fluently speaking the English language. In that regard, I will inevitably discuss some of the musical artists and songwriters who opened up the Anglo-Saxon culture to him. I, naturally, will talk about how, at an early young age, Onkere came across the English language in Toshville, Mpugu. I will then talk about his primary and high school experiences before underlining his years as a college student in the English Department of his country of origin in Africa.

I then will discuss his experience as a college student at Regina University in Europe and how, from there, he went on to successfully pursue his studies in the United States of America. His different experiences in America will ineluctably be commented upon. His years spent at Charles-Raymond University, both as a teaching assistant (TA) and as a student, will be discussed prior to talking about his experience as an instructor of English and principles of communication at Eliriga University in America. I will close the experience chapter discussing his teachings as assistant professor of English and American studies at the national university of his country of origin in Africa.

His experience at the Great Organization in Washington, DC, as an adviser will be highlighted, stressing how his understanding and mastering of the English language would be used to loyally serve and represent his country at one of the highest levels of international diplomacy. The narrator will not use real names of people who helped our main character along the way on his journey. In order to avoid any libel and privacy issues, the names of primary and secondary schools, together with colleges, universities, associations, and organizations, are out of the author's fabrication.

It is important for the readers to know that the author of the present narration possesses a bachelor's degree in English and two master's degrees in both French and Francophone world studies and English. He holds a doctorate in English and American studies. Those degrees were respectively conferred to him by prestigious African, European, and American universities. The author is first and foremost a university professor who has taught French, English, and American and communication studies for many years in American, European, and African universities. He speaks more than two international languages, on top of the African ones that he can speak as well. He is also a seasoned diplomat currently working for an international organization. The author has been married for almost ten years and has four remarkable children.

In the final analysis, this story is all about education, languages, culture, identity, character building, and how a young determined boy from Akaga City, a city located in the northeastern province of Haute-Savana in Africa, turned out to realize his dream of skillfully mastering not only the English language but also American culture.

CHAPTER 1

Encounter with the English Language: Fefe

A dream doesn't become reality through magic;
it takes sweat, determination, and hard work.
—Colin Powell

THE ENGLISH LANGUAGE

A traditional African wooden house with walls all boldly covered with layers of some sort of brownish mud—that is the house Onkere grew up in. Its roof, even though made with metal sheet, was also covered in part with a local material referred to as thatch. While the front and unique entrance door was made of a wooden material, its windows were essentially made from bamboo material. The small house had three sorts of bedrooms without any type of living room whatsoever. The family had no television, nor any of the furniture used in modern houses. Onkere would go watch television at the local retailer's grocery store, where its owner would turn it off almost immediately after the national hymn was sung. The neighborhood the protagonist grew up in was very noisy, with pubs around almost every corner. By the time Onkere was born, there were no water installations in his family house. Family members would collect rainwater from the open sky through cleaned containers, and it would be boiled to make it drinkable. Whenever it rained, the protagonist would go out to play with his little friends. The electricity was not equally shared in Akaga City, either. Young adolescent boys and girls older than Onkere, around the early seventies, would hang out under the utility poles to enjoy the light. Some high school students would most likely spend time under the utility poles at night, going over their lessons, because their folks were too poor to afford electricity at home. People Onkere grew up around in Akaga City were very friendly.

Akaga City is a small African town of more than one thousand people located in the northeastern province of Haute-Savana, Mpugu, a French-speaking country located in West Africa. Nowadays, Akaga City is a sort of modernized village where houses are built for the most part with concrete material, cement, and wood. The village has about three main roads leading to the neighboring major villages and cities. Houses are basically built on both sides of the roads. This characteristic, in itself, strengthens bonds among the community, whereby everyone knows everyone. Akaga City is famous for its splendid exotic palm, coconut, papaya, and mango trees that are easily seen along the roads. Now and then, unattended dogs, goats, or she-goats could be perceived running all over the place, especially upon hearing the honk of an old bus or car. Grocery stores are built, as well, on each side of the main dusty roads. This allows travelers going through the village to observe its traditional markets where local women exhibit their merchandise and agricultural products covered with dust. By the time Onkere was born, Akaga City's roads were still unpaved. Thus, the houses built near them would be full of dusty brownish roofs that would turn gray after the passage of the rain. At nighttime, mothers would drag their nude kids to the public fountain to give them baths. Onkere himself went through that process while growing up. By the time he was about three years old, cars and buses were still unusual sights in the village. Whenever kids would see one, it would be an amazing spectacle to watch, as they would run after the slow-moving bus or car, which, for the most part, would be dropping passengers off from one village to the next one.

While growing up, Onkere enjoyed eating a local vegetable called *nkumu*. He also liked to eat cassava, as well as coconut, bananas, and mangoes, eating habits he had received from his father. Monray was Onkere's father's real name. Yet he was referred to as Mister. He was the eldest of his family. He had three sisters and two brothers. Born around the thirties, Monray dreamed of pursuing studies at a university level. However, given that he was the eldest of his family, he had, at a very young age, given up his dream in order to take care of his family, his beautiful wife, and his amazing children. Right after completing primary school, he got married to Onkere's mother, Mrs. Monray, whose birth name was Tassina. She was born around the forties. She was part of a typical, traditional African family composed of three daughters, herself included, and three sons.

We were originally twelve children. Some have gone to heaven and are sitting by the Lord's right hand now. As for me, Onkere, I am the seventh child out of that number. I happen to be the middle child. In some world cultures, being the middle child has implications that will be discussed later on. I was born in Akaga City. My father's quest for employment opportunities led him to move the family to Toshville, the capital city of the Haute-Savana province.

It would be in Toshville that I attended primary and secondary schools. When I was still in primary school, in the late 1980s, when I probably was a third grader, one of my twin sisters, Mariella, was dating a nicely brilliant young man by the name of Fefe. He was good natured and physically attractive. He enjoyed getting well dressed. Tall and thin, he walked in a graceful way that would synchronize all his body while in motion. Full of energy and gently mannered, Fefe was intensely in love with my sister. The two of them were almost inseparable. They enjoyed publicly showing off their affection for each other.

This was an unusual occurrence in Toshville during those years. Mariella was as tall as her boyfriend. She was as equally smart. She was a strong-willed person who would not accept no for an answer. Her very long, thin molten-red hair would nicely fall over her shoulder, to the amazement of her boyfriend. She enjoyed eating wild fruits and was quick to throw up upon smelling something rotten. She was caring and very sensitive. Like her twin sister, Olivia, Mariella was well mannered. She was a feminist of some sort.

During this period of time, Michael Jackson, the iconic American pop artist, had already successfully released his 1983 *Thriller* album that would make him win a Grammy

Award a year later. In Toshville, there was a frenzied enthusiasm about his music. Every single little boy wanted to sing, dance, walk, and moonwalk just like him.

Madonna was also one of the most liked American pop stars. In fact, my other twin sister, Olivia, used to dress just the way Madonna would. Olivia excessively loved also to dance to Madonna's "Who's That Girl" song. Olivia was a remarkable person with a very unique taste in music and American pop culture. She was bright and affectionate yet sneaky. She was as tall as her twin sister, Mariella, with whom she shared an unusual sensitiveness when it came to matters love related. She did not appreciate drunk persons being around her. Olivia, who was of a darker skin color than her twin sister, had what is referred to as long, thin ebony-black hair, which would tenderly sit on her shoulder. Both Olivia and her twin sister had ladylike personalities that could scare off young men lacking certain confidence or boldness.

Fefe was already a junior in Toshville public high school. As such, he had already been learning English—a foreign language—for about three or four years. And he was excellent at it. Not only could he dance and walk like Michael Jackson, but he, above all, could sing Michael Jackson's songs because he knew English and had certainly—as I can now think about it—studied and learned the lyrics.

Singing Michael Jackson's songs and practicing his moves were part of how some young men came to impress young women of that generation. As for Onkere, he not only loved his sister Mariella, as well as Olivia, but appreciated more the fact that Fefe could fluently speak English, even though, in the early 1980s, Onkere, being too young and full of naivete, did not know that the language his brother-in-law was speaking was called English.

In fact, one day, Fefe went to their house to visit his girlfriend, Mariella. Fortunately for him, their father was out to work, as he always was. Mister was very protective of his twins. He did not want them to be dating anyone who could potentially derail them from focusing on school. Mister, to describe him, was a medium-sized, good-looking, stocky man who could scare off men of his generation.

A story is even told according to which Mister, who actually never underwent any type of football training, was a cook whose career started with him working for an embassy in Bonneville, Mpugu's capital city. As time passed by, Daddy Monray, as he was also called by some of his colleagues, switched from that embassy to working for some private school. Midway through his career, he finally went to work for Mpugu's football team. Given that he was older than the majority of the young energetic men, some of them were mean to Daddy Monray. To punish those young men, Daddy Monray, being the chef in charge of supervising restaurants and any related food service devoted to feeding athletes to keep them healthy and ready for any type of activities, would purposely reduce the number of supplies as well as any daily food ration allocated to those specific football players.

The young men impacted by Daddy Monray's action would get frustrated with him. Consequently, they would openly look for any chance to challenge him to fights.

Daddy Monray, knowing that he still had a violent knockout punch, would purposely turn them down. But given that they would insist, one day, out of the blue, during one of the many arguments he would occasionally have with those young men, Daddy Monray, like a lion about to catch its prey, jumped on one of them. Nobody knows what happened next. From that day forward though, Daddy Monray, regardless of what went down on that day, was forever respected among those young athletes who thought that because they had been trained as military men, they could easily scare him off. Following this event, a song came out celebrating Daddy Monray's strength.

Daddy Monray, despite this misunderstanding and many more, would gently interact with people in his dealings. His temperament was successfully passed down to all his children, especially Onkere, whose mother was a more reserved and privately quiet lady who would not hurt a bird. She certainly was somewhere in the kitchen or had gone grocery shopping when Fefe came in. Onkere's other sister Olivia was at home, while his brother Randy was out, as usual. At this stage, the Monray family was made up of seven children: Eyila, the eldest, the twin sisters, Mariella and Olivia, Randy, Onkere himself, and his two little sisters, Yogi and Dah.

The day Fefe came to our house, almost everybody was out except for Mariella, Olivia, my mother, and I. Fefe, I remember, came straight from school because he still had the school uniform on. Once in, he started speaking to my sister in a language I did not know existed. My sister Mariella could understand some of it because she was a junior at the same public high school her boyfriend was attending. I cannot remember hearing her practicing it at home. Impressed with Fefe's speaking ability to perform the language, I asked him right away in French—obviously— the following questions.

7

"What kind of language is this, Fefe?"

"It's English!" he answered.

"Can I speak it?"

"Oh yes! For that to happen, you need to finish primary school and graduate to attend any high school where this foreign language is taught."

The exchange between Fefe and Onkere, before the latter knew it, was going to be the determining factor that would actively motivate the young boy from Akaga City to literally chase the English language for years. Onkere was so impressed with the way Fefe sounded while skillfully speaking this beautiful language, whose existence he was just discovering, that he kept dreaming that day about being able to comfortably speak that language, one day, as excellently as Fefe. Right there on the spot, following the exchange, he promised Fefe that, yes, he would undoubtedly and unquestionably graduate from primary school and attend any high school in the country to get a chance to be taught this beautiful language, English, he had just fallen in love with.

CHAPTER 2

Mr. James Jones

Learn everything you can, anytime you can,
from anyone you can; there will always come
a time when you will be grateful you did.
—Sarah Caldwell

KABANA PUBLIC HIGH SCHOOL

The year that followed the previously mentioned exchange between Fefe and Onkere, the latter did everything he could to be around Fefe so he could pick some English words and vocabulary. And, little by little, as he expected, before he knew it, he had gradually started to learn how to introduce himself in English. He noticeably learned the basics from Fefe. Two years after his first encounter with the English language, Onkere, as promised, successfully graduated from primary school and went on to Kabana Public High School in Toshville. The idea of attending that public high school really made him feel some sort of good and pride about himself, because he fully knew he would be able to have the opportunity to finally learn English.

As it turned out, around that time in the early 1990s, coincidentally, the American Peace Corps, created by President John F. Kennedy around 1961, was still profusely sending talented young American volunteers around the world. Thus, around 1989 or 1990, some of these remarkably high-spirited young American Peace Corps volunteers were sent to Africa, especially to Mpugu to help students learn English. Among the American volunteers who came to Kabana Public High School were Mr. James Jones, his wife, Annette Jones, and Ms. Ballwalter.

I must confess that I am not 100 percent certain about their names' spelling given that I was about thirteen or fourteen years old. I am also not sure if they were from Pennsylvania or Boston. One thing is definitely sure; they were enthusiastic young Americans who came straight from America.

Of these three American Peace Corps volunteers, Mr. Jones was assigned to our class. When the fall semester started, Onkere was uncontrollably more than excited. Yet, strangely enough, he was eerily apprehensive about meeting his English instructor and nervous about how the first encounter, on which would depend the rest of his love story to English, would go.

We had already been given the schedule, and I knew that we would have an English class on Mondays, Wednesdays, and Fridays. I could not sleep on the eve of my first day of school. Many ideas were confusingly going through my head. However, when that first day of my English class came, I made sure I would get to class on time, which I did.

Pretty much, newcomers and old students were packed in the class waiting for the English teacher to come in. I believe he showed up some fifteen minutes past time because I remember Onkere getting agitatedly annoyed. He kept asking when the instructor was going to show up. Finally, when Mr. Jones showed up, everybody suddenly stood up. He warmly greeted all of us in a baritone voice.

"Good morning, class. My name is Mr. Jones. I am your English teacher."

The entire class, including Onkere, synchronically responded. "Good morning, sir!"

He then asked all of us to sit down, which we did. Mr. Jones was a very tall man, about seven feet tall, like Shaquille O'Neal. He was not originally an English instructor but a mathematician whose favorite sport was basketball. He had very short brown, curvy hair, and he would always sparse his hair with his hand. He was a very open-minded instructor who liked to joke around to make students feel more comfortable. He had a cheerful personality. Yet he could get mad quickly if students were not paying attention. On that first day, the lesson covered was the English alphabet and its subsequent song.

At the end of the day of his encounter with the English instructor, Onkere blessed God for sending Mr. Jones, a highly-spirited and enthusiastic American man, full of energy, to be the first English teacher he would have. Was it luck or fate?

As the months passed by, Onkere gradually developed a kind of personal solid friendship with Mr. and Mrs. Jones. Mr. Jones was so tall that when he walked, he would dangle. In fact, we did walk many times because, obviously, the

Jones did not own cars. They lived about twenty minutes away from Kabana Public High School.

During the first year of Onkere's sixth grade, needless to say, he was Mr. Jones's best student. Because of that fact, Mr. Jones would proudly brag about him to his wife and Ms. Ballwalter, the other two young American Peace Corps volunteers. Both of these ladies were teaching seventh and eighth grades. I can only assume that they too would say a few words to Mr. Jones about some of their best students. Among those was a certain student by the name of Roddy. He was three levels above Onkere. As such, he was a little older than our main protagonist. This also means that Roddy had already been studying English for about three years. As a matter of fact, he was in ninth grade, while the young boy from Akaga City was just beginning sixth grade. Roddy was a tall, thin, light boy who had long legs to a point where when he walked, it felt like he was dragging them. He was a nice-looking young man with a bubbly personality. He loved to laugh out loud. He was full of joy and had a remarkable passion for the English language.

I had heard about Roddy and how amazingly fluent he was in English. I was already looking for ways to meet with him.

As it turned out, my wish would be fulfilled when, one Saturday afternoon, I paid Mr. and Mrs. Jones a visit. And right there, Roddy was already at their place along with Ms. Ballwalter. Naturally, I joined them and was introduced to Roddy. It was a shiny, nice afternoon during which a lot of small talks were done. It was during that same day that I also met and exchanged words with Ms. Ballwalter for the first time. Ms. Ballwalter was as tall as Mr. Jones. She had long, thin brown hair that fell to almost her slender waist. She had a nice smile that would mesmerize people around her whenever she cracked a joke. She was the youngest among the volunteers. As such, she seemed very joyful, with a bubbly personality as well.

As for Mr. Jones's wife, Annette, she was the smallest of the three. She had long, thin, dark hair that fell over her shoulder. Given that she was married, she appeared to be a very reserved, soft-spoken yet strong-willed person. She was bright and knew what was best for her husband and herself. She was persuasive when she wanted to be. She genuinely was a good listener and a person to seek advice from. She had slender eyebrows that would give the impression that she had eye issues, especially given that she wore glasses from time to time, just like her husband.

My solid friendship with the Joneses lasted for two years because they had to return to the United States around 1991 or 1992, I believe. During the two years I got to intensively socialize with them, I was not only properly familiarized with the English language, and particularly American English, but I was also exposed to American culture as a whole. Socializing with the Joneses allowed me, for example, to greatly appreciate American folk and pop music. I was exposed to numerous pop songwriters and singers. Among them, to name a few were Edie Brickell, Pete Seeger, Jim Croce, Peter, Paul, and Mary, Bob Dylan, Kenny Rogers, Dan Seals, Sam Cooke, Don Williams, Dolly Parton, and John Denver. We would spend time listening to songs like Dylan's "Blowin' in the Wind," Jim Croce's "Time in a Bottle," Edie Brickell's "What I Am," Dolly Parton's "Coat of Many Colors," Denver's "Leaving on a Jet Plane," Sam Cooke's

"Don't Know Much about History," and Don Williams's "Listen to the Radio." The Joneses and Ms. Ballwalter were all musically inclined. They introduced American music to me. As for Onkere, American music brought an added value on top of the simple fact of listening to it. He would work on writing down the lyrics of these songs and many more before having them proofread by the Joneses. Through that learning process, he consciously developed and kept building his vocabulary while simultaneously improving his efficiency and hearing abilities.

By 1993, he had learned many of these songs by heart and would sing some of them out of memory. Singing songs in English became a tool that would ultimately allow him to measure any improvement made as related to his way of sounding and pronouncing words. In order to help him successfully accomplish this goal, Mr. Jones had provided him with a small English dictionary to help him check out expressions as well as their spelling and phonetic transcription.

As weird as this might sound, Onkere pretty much would use that dictionary to check out every new word he discovered through writing down song lyrics. Even weirder was the fact that he jealously kept that dictionary by his bedside and would only fall asleep after having checked and learned new words or expressions out of it. Some could argue that that particular dictionary became his Bible, while others might as well suggest it became his Koran. As for him, it was an invaluable source of knowledge. Still, around 1993, there was no internet to Google words, let alone YouTube where he could check out words and expressions. Moreover, there were no such devices as iPhones or cell phones where he could get connected to the internet and do research.

Onkere was also introduced to some important songs symbolizing the civil rights movement, such as "We Shall Overcome," "Nobody Knows the Trouble I've Seen," and "Lift Every Voice and Sing," even though he never discussed the civil rights movement with the Joneses or Ms. Ballwalter. Retrospectively, I realize that the Joneses and Ms. Ballwalter could not have discussed this kind of subject with Onkere because he was too young to grasp what they would be talking about. Remember, the discussion would have been in English, and I am not sure he would have gotten the kind of vocabulary necessarily associated with that movement.

Nevertheless, Onkere really learned as much as he could from the Joneses. Many of the American cultural aspects he was learning were taught to him outside of the classrooms. While the Joneses were teaching him anything they possibly could, they were, however, clear and always reminded him not to neglect the other subjects. They pretty much demanded him to be as good at the rest of the subjects being taught in school. To that requirement, he did the best he could.

Apart from discussing and listening to the music appreciated by the Joneses and Ms. Ballwalter, we would also discuss other aspects of American culture. Some days, the discussions would be about culinary art. Some other days, they would be about basketball or American soccer games. On some other occasions, they would teach Onkere how to pronounce certain specific words and expressions. The Joneses would teach him vocabulary related to almost any aspect and sector of activity likely to have an impact on human beings.

It's clear to me now that prior to 1992, the year they probably returned to America, the Joneses' mission, when it came to their relationship with Onkere, was to build up his vocabulary. And of course, he was willing and able to learn and use it whenever he got a chance to do so. Being friend with the Joneses and Ms. Ballwalter also allowed him to necessarily practice English more than his classmates. One understands why he would always try the best he could to sound just like the Joneses. He knew he had to keep working at it, practicing to hopefully get to some kind of perfection. He was vehemently determined to fluently speak English, and all he wanted to do was keeping learning and practicing it.

As the year of their departure neared, I remember I was already in seventh grade, and Mr. Jones, who had now become a mentor to me, had numerous small talks and discussions with me. During one of our discussions, he told me—I do not know if he really meant it—that he could take Onkere back with him to America. But, given that the latter was still a minor, he would eventually have to discuss the idea with his parents, mainly Mister, Onkere's father.

If he agreed with the idea, then Mr. Jones would gladly go to their place to meet with him to discuss the issue. Needless to say, I was overjoyed and very excited about the prospect to see Onkere travel to America and live his own experiences about everything we had been abundantly learning and discussing with the Joneses and Ms. Ballwalter for about two straight years.

The idea of Onkere leaving his parents for America around 1992 when I was about fourteen years old was short-lived. Unfortunately, it did not fly. Mister vehemently rejected it. As for me, I hated Onkere's father for that. In fact, I remained mad at both of his parents for more than a month. Eventually, my anger went away, and life went on. I would never know how Onkere reacted to his father's decision. We never had a chance to discuss the case once Mister made it clear to him that it was a classified case.

When the Joneses and Ms. Ballwalter finally left Toshville for America, they left us—Onkere included—with grammar books, dictionaries, audio tapes, music tapes, pretty much anything they did not need but knew would help us improve our English skills. Needless to say, I socialized with the Joneses and Ms. Ballwalter, and, like Onkere, I was more than saddened by their departure.

CHAPTER 3

English Club: Leadership on the Rise

Leadership and Learning are indispensable to each other.
—John F. Kennedy

O&R PRIVATE HIGH SCHOOL

After the Joneses and Ms. Ballwalter left Toshville, two major changes happened. First, as Onkere did not want to pursue a career as a high school instructor, which could have happened had he remained at Kabana Public High School, he left and went to O&R Private High School where he was accepted in eighth grade.

For two years, from sixth to seventh grade, he was taught English by a charismatic, motivational native speaker named Mr. Jones, whose entourage was made up of incredible native speakers, whose way of eloquently speaking and sounding I came to idealize. Now Onkere found himself at O&R being taught English by nonnative speakers. He had, therefore, to rapidly adjust to that new reality, which constituted the second big change.

During his first year at O&R Private High School as an eighth grader, the protagonist had Mr. Noan as his English instructor. Mr. Noan was in his early fifties, if I am not mistaken. He was originally from a Central African country, which name I have forgotten. He was very knowledgeable and stressed to us the importance of understanding and mastering English grammar. During his tenure, Onkere improved his grammatical skills while always working on his capacity to orally express himself. Mr. Noan had black, curvy, short hair. He wore glasses, which was indicative of him having eye issues. He loved to get well dressed. As an instructor, he was strict. He knew how to crack jokes just to make students participate in class activities. He had a strong personality, so much so that his presence in class demanded attention.

Moreover, during that first year, there was a student as good at English as was Onkere. His name was Richy. During Mr. Noan's class, Richy and Onkere would go back and forth challenging each other to better themselves at becoming the best at English. Grades scored during tests would ultimately serve as a measurement of their abilities and skills in writing the English language. On some tests, Richy would score higher than Onkere. On some others, the trend would be reversed. Richy was taller than Onkere. He was also of a lighter skin color than was the protagonist. He always liked to be well dressed. Richy had a strong personality. As Onkere, he too liked listening to music and reading good books.

In order to keep improving his way of fluently speaking English, given that Onkere always wanted to sound like his mentor, Mr. Jones, he kept trying to sound like him years after the latter returned to America. In the meantime, as months passed by, Richy and I came up with the idea of creating and ultimately managing an English Club that would be beneficial to students attending O&R Private High School. Needless to say, Richy and I, by this time, had already struck up a solid friendship. We discussed the idea for a while among ourselves and ended up deciding to submit an outline and program to our English instructor, who had the monumental responsibility and the authority to convince the director and the administrative personnel of the school to give us the okay to set up such a club. As it turned out, the idea was approved, and Richy and I were given permission to open an English Club. Onkere would use all the documents, books, audio tapes, recordings, and dictionaries he had inherited from the Joneses and Ms. Ballwalter as the basis that would allow us to manage the English Club under the supervision of our instructor, Mr. Noan.

Basically, the English Club was an opportunity and a platform where any student from any high school could join to improve their English skills. The idea was very simple.

Richy and I would learn song lyrics and teach them to the rest of the students enrolled in the club. We would listen to songs in English and go about explaining the context and lyrics to the club members. Occasionally, we would also help them with their home assignments. Since we were in charge, Richy and I had the moral obligation to be really excellent at English, willing and able to explain the slightest grammatical nuance in a sentence or out of a text if need be.

The club had a choir. Richy and Onkere were in charge of picking and teaching choir members the songs to be performed during the school shows. Some of the songs the choir would perform were gospel songs such as "Nobody Knows the Trouble I've Seen," "When the Saints Go Marchin' In," and "We Shall Overcome" and pop songs such as "This Land Is My Land" and "Blowin' in the Wind." I had the chance to know both Richy and Onkere during the period of time being narrated. Consequently, I attended many of their rehearsals and enjoyed on more than one occasion seeing the choir perform the above-mentioned songs.

I furthermore enjoyed watching them performing songs by Phil Collins such as "Another Day in Paradise" and "Do You Remember," songs by Tracy Chapman such as "Fast Car" and "Talkin' about a Revolution," and even Bob Marley's "Redemption Song."

Because of the slight notoriety that comes with leading and managing an English Club in a French-speaking setting, among French-speaking students, Richy and Onkere became well-known by the school's board of directors. But, most importantly to these two eighth graders, their leadership abilities and skills were known and respected by their peers. I was almost fifteen years old. I remember this vividly. Words about two excellent young eighth graders speaking beautiful English spread like wildfire.

The following year, Richy and I both moved up to ninth grade. We kept managing the English Club's activities. Mr. Theo would be our new English instructor this time around. He, too, was from an African country located probably in the horn of the continent. Mr. Theo was very strict as an instructor. The reality is that, for some reason, I was scared of him because rumor had it that he had no patience whatsoever with students. As a result, I honestly was nervous and was very apprehensive about the first day of class.

Fortunately for me, my fame—or more precisely, my reputation—had preceded me. My skills and abilities in the English language were already known by him. As it turned out, Richy and I ended up being not only his best students but his friends as well. As a matter of fact, Mr. Theo would go tell his twelfth graders, more advanced than Richy and Onkere, that the latter had reached a level of mastering the English language far more advanced than theirs—and that Onkere could even teach English to them. This kind of story would be reported to Onkere by Mr. Theo's twelfth-grade students themselves. Among these were Little and Fab, who both ended up being dear friends of mine—and are to this day.

Little and I lived in the same neighborhood. I looked up to him for advice most of the time because he knew a lot of things I did not know and made himself available to me. Little was very friendly. He was also an open-minded type of person who knew how to get ladies' attention. Little was a thin, light-skinned young man. His female classmates were, for the most part, attracted to him because he had read numerous novels examining French romanticism and poetry. This means that he spoke French beautifully, and girls were amazingly attracted to that feature as well. More than that, I truly appreciated the fact that Little would step up to the plate to protect the neighborhood kids from any outside threats coming from surrounding gang squads. I learned a lot from Little about how to handle some mean-spirited girls. From our friendship, I developed a passion for French romanticism and poetry.

Fab was as tall and skinny as Little. They were classmates yet did not know each other until I introduced them. Fab was a very laid-back type of person who knew how to defuse tense crises that broke out among students or between students and administrative personnel.

As a matter of fact, there used to be a national championship football game. Throughout the country, high schools had teams compete and challenge one another so that the two best teams from respective high schools got to face off during the finale. O&R Private High School had a football team, which my other friend Ziguy was a member of. For some reasons that I no longer can remember, the head coach in charge of training our team kept Ziguy off during one of the most important games of the season, knowing full well that he was the best player of the team, thus its star athlete. Ziguy, who was unhappy with the whole situation, uttered words about doing something to the head coach if the latter did not let him play, which he did not. As the game was gradually nearing to the first half, seeing that the head coach was not budging, Ziguy, who lived some four or five blocks away, across the street from the high school, made it clear that he was going to his place to get nobody knew what and that he would return doing nobody knew what to the head coach. Fab was one of the leading students, myself included, who tried to reason with Ziguy and persuade him not to pursue whatever endeavor he was thinking of at that precise moment. Given that the event happened in an open space, a football field full of students on a sunny afternoon, all the students and administrative authorities were alerted. There was confusion everywhere. It felt like chaos.

Never in the history of O&R Private High School had such a situation happened. Questions were being asked. Was he serious? Did he have what it took to carry out whatever he was thinking of doing? Could his friends stop him? What would happen next?

To shorten the story, let me say that his friends followed him to his place and courageously succeeded in calming him down. He cooled off and never returned to school that day. He was suspended for a while but was eventually accepted back to class. His parents could have sued the school, arguing that they were paying for their son to attend O&R and demanding full reimbursement in case he was expelled. However, thanks to Fab, Richy, me, and other classmates, what could have led to who knows what, maybe a tragedy of some sort, was eventually prevented.

Leading the English Club into the second year, Richy and I decided to make a public presentation to show what we had been doing. The entire school was informed about our intent to have a show at the end of the school year. That same year, we worked hard and made sure the audience would enjoy the show. We knew that the director, the students, and the entire administrative personnel would be present. Our awareness suggested that students would also come from other high schools to enjoy the show. It was the show of the year everybody was talking about. That school year, in addition to the songs and Negro spirituals that would be presented by the choir, Richy and Onkere had to make individual oratory presentations on any topic of their choosing. I decided to make mine on Dr. Martin Luther

King Jr.'s "I Have a Dream" speech. I studied it carefully and memorized every little passage, pause, and comma contained in the speech so that Dr. King himself would be so graciously generous to congratulate me from above at the end of my performance.

Truth be told, I was especially thankful to the Joneses and Ms. Ballwalter, who had left us with incredible documents I was now using to the benefit of an entire community of parents, students, and educators.

Onkere remained in close contact with the Joneses right after they left Toshville. They kept in touch writing each other. They would send him packages. He would gleefully get them and let everyone around him know that the packages came from America and were from the Joneses. He would then unwrap them and discover what it was all about. If my memory serves me right, I believe he received three or four of those packages. They all contained dictionaries and grammar and idiom books.

They sometimes contained books with imagery as well as great vocabulary. In one of the packages, the Joneses sent him his first book on Dr. Martin Luther King Jr., whose title I cannot remember. All I can recall is that it was a voluminous book, about six hundred pages, for which Onkere was delightfully happy. It contained some of the major speeches delivered by Dr. Martin Luther King Jr., which would be mimicked years later by Onkere, among which was the "I Have a Dream" speech.

The day of the show finally came. As expected, the English Club choir made a remarkable performance. The choir, which Richy, Onkere, and I were part of, sang some Negro spirituals together with some gospel and pop songs.

Here again, the choir sang "Nobody Knows the Trouble I've Seen" and "When the Saints Go Marchin' In." The choir also sang "Five Hundred Miles" and "This Land Is Your Land." Richy, Onkere, and I closed the performances singing Phil Collins's "Another Day in Paradise" and "Do You Remember." The choir did a heck of a good job. The performers sang in harmony. Each move and gesture was beautifully rehearsed and synchronized.

There was, at the end of the show that lasted about two and a half hours, a feeling of ecstasy coming from the audience. All the performers felt it. I felt it. Onkere felt it. Richy felt it too. So did Onkere's sisters.

By the time of the show, Yogi and Dah had already joined the English Club's choir and, therefore, were part of that unforgettable night. They were actually among the choir's very first members. The show, I have been told, went down in the school history as being one of the best shows ever organized.

As for my solo performance that same day, as could have been expected out of me, I made an amazingly outstanding oratory presentation. I skillfully exhibited my oratory abilities in mastering the English language for everybody to see. I brilliantly mimicked Dr. King's speech. Richy delivered the best performance of his life as well. It is safe to say that our performances were equally matched.

From that day forward, I tried to learn anything I possibly could about Dr. Martin Luther King Jr. By this time, I was already familiar with his fight and nonviolence philosophy. I had already been introduced to him by Mister himself, in addition to the book and documents I had on Dr. Martin Luther King Jr. Onkere's father is the one who, one day, while watching a documentary about apartheid in South Africa, made a point about the fact that there was an African American young man named Dr. Martin Luther King Jr. who, before Mandela's fight started to become internationally known, had also fought against segregation and racial prejudice in order to better African Americans as well as poor whites' life conditions. It is safe to say that Mister had a solid worldview knowledge that allowed him to comprehend issues some twenty-first-century university graduate students would not be able to grasp.

By the time I moved to tenth grade, Mister had already been paying for Onkere's education for two years. By that time, two family members had been added to the Monray existing ones. Onkere still had three brothers, himself included.

But the number of his sisters had increased to seven. Opy and Claudia had been now part of the picture for a while, and Opy more so than Claudia.

His father was still earning, on a monthly basis, what could be perceived in today's standards as a meager salary. Almost half of that money was spent on paying for Onkere's education. The new and additional responsibilities that came with providing for the protagonist's two little sisters did not allow his father to keep up with financing his studies. As a consequence, he had to, once again, move to another high school upon completing ninth grade. This time around, Mister got in touch with one of his many relatives, Mr. Doine, who had some sort of authority within the national department of education. He fraternally asked him to find ways to enroll both Onkere and his brother Randy in Toshville Public High School. Fortunately for the two brothers, they were accepted, Randy to twelfth grade and Onkere to tenth grade. Randy, who had a winning personality, was very bright and a quick thinker. He exemplified calmness and boldness and was as determined as his junior brother Onkere. Randy was fun to be around, as he showed leadership abilities to everyone who knew him. He enjoyed intellectual debates as much as his brother did. His presence in a room demanded attention, even though he knew the world did not revolve around him. He was someone the protagonist would gladly seek advice of any sort from.

One of the changes that occurred with this move of ours was that Richy, whom I had become close to, and I went our separate ways, even if we did the best we could to remain friends. Going our separate ways was hard on both of us. But I had to do what I had to. While I was at O&R Private High School, and because our first names sounded slightly alike, people would sometimes mistake me for Richy and vice versa. As birds of the same feather flock together, he and I were always together: Richy and Onkere. The latter was also known as Riky during that period of time.

The reality was that during those two years spent at O&R Private High School, Richy and Riky did not always approach things the same way over leadership. They had a few misunderstandings about who was best at managing the English Club. That being said, they always came to terms with each other.

At this stage, Ziguy had been a friend to both Richy and Riky. He loved reggae music, especially Bob Marley's songs. He was taller than both Richy and Riky. He liked to dress very nicely. Because of him being tall like a model, good-looking, and full of a positive attitude, girls were always attracted to him. They would literally fight over him, and he knew it. Ziguy had the cream of the cream in terms of ladies. We liked to hang out with him and be among famous people, so to speak. Richy and Riky would also use Ziguy to settle misunderstandings between them. As always, his advice to them regarding any trouble over a girl, for example, was that whoever was not picked, in the final analysis, had to accept the verdict rendered by the one member of the jury—the girl at the center of the misunderstanding.

Because of his commitment to justice, equity, and fairness, Richy and Riky enjoyed hanging out with Ziguy, who was really into fashion and clothing. On top of being a football star, he was lucky enough to have sisters who could provide him with any brand-new type of shoes, clothes, or watches he so desired.

TOSHVILLE PUBLIC HIGH SCHOOL

I, like Onkere, was nervous the day I started my tenth-grade English class. Five minutes into waiting for the instructor, a six-foot-tall, black, handsome man entered the class. He introduced himself as being Mr. Kaku. He pointed out that he was—strictly from an African cultural standpoint—uncle to his students. Unlike my two former English instructors, both from foreign African countries, Mr. Kaku, like myself, was from Mpugu. A London-trained English instructor originally from the Haute-Savana province, Mr. Kaku's origin and family background made me feel a sense of pride and brotherhood. Mr. Kaku had brownish, thin hair. He enjoyed smoking a manlike type of cigarette. He spoke English with a very distinctive British diction.

Not only could Onkere understand English, but more importantly, he and I could speak Mr. Kaku's maternal language. This sense of linguistic proximity made me, as well as Onkere, feel more comfortable with Mr. Kaku. He was one of us, one of our own, who, like Onkere's instructors before him, would stress the importance of mastering the English grammar. Pretty much every lesson we ended up learning was a grammatically based one. We also read extracts from different authors and genres. Many of the readings came from British authors.

During this period of time, in my English class, there was a student as brilliant as Onkere. His name was Dylan. He came straight from my hometown of Akaga City. Like Onkere and myself, he had been trained by American instructors who came through the program that brought the Joneses and Ms. Ballwalter, three years earlier, to Toshville. Dylan was as tall as Mr. Kaku. He was a soft-spoken person with a strong will. He knew what he wanted and when he wanted it. His presence, anywhere, demanded attention, and he knew how to nicely get it. He was a quiet person who could be talkative when need be. He was a quick thinker who had ebony hair.

Dylan and Onkere would go about it for two years, just like he and Richy went about it for the same amount of years. Unlike Richy, who sounded British, Dylan sounded more like an American.

There had been a consistency in him working toward keeping that beautiful accent. Like Onkere and I, he was familiar with American culture and pop music. His American instructor, whose name I cannot remember, had provided him with documents and audio tapes just like the Joneses and Ms. Ballwalter did for Onkere and me. More importantly, Dylan passionately loved the English language. He eagerly wanted to be the best at it. As a consequence, he did whatever he could to remain the best. Understandably so, he was naturally competitive with Onkere, as I can only imagine the latter was with him. Having Dylan in class made Onkere want to remain on top of his game as well. As the months went by, Mr. Kaku, who had become so proud of Onkere for his abilities in the English language, publicly bragged about him to his Nigerian and Ghanaian friends. He told them straight up that he had a student—Onkere— who could easily have long conversations with them.

As a former French colony, Mpugu is a French-speaking country. Therefore, as French speakers, English does not come effortlessly to people from Mpugu. By the same token, English does not come straightforwardly to anybody whose official language is French. Reversely, the argument could be made that French does not come easily to English or American speakers.

In both cases, fluently speaking and correctly writing one or the other language requires some practice and learning of grammatical aspects and pronunciation ramifications. Maybe that could help explain why Mr. Kaku was so proud of his best students, which Dylan, Onkere, and I were part of.

One day, all of a sudden, after school, Mr. Kaku requested Onkere to accompany him to see his friends. They boarded a cab and went to join Mr. Kaku's friends from the above-mentioned English-speaking countries. They notably joined his Nigerian friends that day. They were businessmen working in Toshville market stores downtown. Once there, he presented Onkere to his friends and brought up a subject, which I no longer can remember. The objective was to let Onkere lead the conversation, which he did. At the end of those small talks that took more than an hour, Mr. Kaku told his friends that he was proud of Onkere. He reminded his friends that he just delivered what he apparently had promised them: bringing one of his students to talk with them in English. It needs to be reiterated that his friends were from English-speaking countries, while Onkere was from the French-speaking country of Mpugu. I can only imagine that that day, like Mr. Kaku, Onkere was proud of himself for what he accomplished.

I can also assert on Onkere's behalf that he had tremendous respect for all our English instructors. He particularly learned from each and every one of them what he could to the best of his abilities. Each of them had their own unique style and way of teaching English. All of them undoubtedly added value to Onkere's knowledge.

As the school year drew to its end, Onkere did well not only in English but also in the rest of the subjects, as the Joneses and Ms. Ballwalter had suggested years ago. Therefore, he moved up to eleventh grade.

For another academic year, Mr. Kaku remained our English teacher, while Dylan continued to be Onkere's main challenger on the subject at the center of the story being narrated. There were one or two other students who were good at English. Dylan and Onkere nonetheless did not drop the ball and remained the key players of the game.

Their competition was purely an intellectual one, with the clear intent of pushing each other to perform well.

Our eleventh-grade English class was amazing because we spent more time making oral presentations. Both Dylan and Onkere were good at fluently speaking. Sometimes, consciously or unconsciously, both would get into different squads just because they did not want to have a leadership problem within the group. Dylan was a student who happened to be very religious. He did not look for misunderstandings, and neither did Onkere.

During this time around, my brother Randy and I came to reconnect with one of our cousins, Chris, who would do everything he could to bring us back to our roots—which meant taking us back to Akaga City, from where our family had departed a long time ago. Toshville Public High School was the biggest public high school in the Haute-Savana province. As such, it welcomed students coming from the neighboring counties or cities. Akaga City was one of these cities. My cousin Chris was one of those students who came from Akaga City to attend Toshville Public High School.

Since my family left Akaga City when we were young, my brother Randy and I did not know much about our roots. Onkere's father had taken the whole family to Bonneville, the capital of Mpugu, in the early seventies before returning to Toshville in the early eighties.

Chris, a twelfth grader, had heard about his cousin and his incredible ability to fluently speak English. Chris himself was not bad at languages. English was also one of the languages he liked. One day, my brother and I were invited to attend an event organized by the association of students from Akaga City.

My brother and I, even though both born in Akaga City, did not particularly feel we belonged. It would be Chris's fraternal duty to make us understand and feel as if we belonged. He proceeded by introducing us to the rest of the members of the association. As it turned out, Dylan, Onkere's challenger, believe it or not, was a member of the association even though he was not really involved in its organizational aspects. Being a member of the association meant that Onkere and he were actually from the same town of Akaga City.

Another day, the association, whose main headquarters was in Toshville, decided to go back to Akaga City to showcase, so to speak, some of the sociocultural activities its members had been doing. For that to happen, a show was to be organized. During the show that took place, Onkere decided to make an oral performance, picking among the many texts he had learned. This time around, he performed Dr. King's "I've Been to the Mountaintop" speech. On top of that, he also performed Marvin Gay's "Sexual Healing" song. Because of his extraordinary performance and breathtaking command of the English language, he became the revelation to the audience, the students, and the people from Akaga City who attended the show. Thanks to his performance in the English language, Onkere successfully and gradually reconnected to his roots. At least, that is what I thought.

Once the show was over, people eagerly wanted to approach him or talk with him. Those who were brave enough to strike a conversation that night asked him who he was and whether he really was one of them, which he said he was. Others, more careful, hesitated to approach him. Rather, they used Chris to introduce them to the protagonist.

Even though he was now an eleventh grader who had acquired some experience in learning and practicing the English language, as demonstrated during his latest performance in Akaga City when he was in tenth grade, he nevertheless was not successful in opening an English Club in Toshville Public High School.

Looking back, I now can explain that situation. Number one, Toshville Public High School was, in terms of size, a bigger high school than O&R Private High School. In that regard, no English instructor had spare time to take on the monumental responsibility of supervising us or any student willing to be part of the English Club's leading team. Additionally, there certainly were twelfth graders who were more fluent in English than some of us. Giving us the opportunity to open and be in charge of an English Club could have been perceived as an insult to those twelfth graders.

As the school year drew to its end, things did not work out okay for Onkere. He was held back to eleventh grade. Even though he was inclined to humanities subjects, he also knew that he had to be good at mathematics to maintain his chances of succeeding in high school and moved to the next level up.

However, we—Onkere and I—had come to the realization that we would not waste our time studying it because whatever position we would have in our future life would not be related to that discipline.

With this reality being consciously ingrained in our brains, we came up with the idea of balancing out mathematics with performing excellently well not only in English but also in Spanish, geography, history, philosophy, French, and French literature. In short, in any humanities-related subjects. As for Onkere, all he needed was just to score two and a half out of twenty as a final grade in mathematics to be moved to the next level up. Nevertheless, in a clearheaded manner, he refused to be held to eleventh grade, knowing that all his friends and classmates, including Dylan, had graduated and moved up to twelfth grade.

Onkere's refusal to be held back implied that he had to, once again, switch high schools. He had two options in front of him. Option one: Mister pays for his school and sends him back to O&R Private High School to complete twelfth grade. In case the first option failed, the second one was to travel to Bonneville, the capital, located some 453,601 miles away from his parents, to go pursue his studies. The latter option is what was done. For reasons already discussed, Onkere's father could no longer pay for his studies, given that there were other children to be taken care of. Plus, Onkere was not the only child attending high school. Two years before, his brother Randy brilliantly graduated and traveled to the capital to attend Bonneville University, where he was now a sophomore studying law.

Randy had urgent financial assistance. In addition, their father was also paying small school fees for their sisters Yogi and Dah. Understandably, Onkere, who did not want to constitute a financial burden for his father, went to live with one of his twin sisters, Mariella. By this time, she was married to Beau, and the couple had two wonderful children, a boy and a girl.

CHAPTER 4

Moving to the Capital: Baccalaureate

If my mind can conceive it,
My heart can believe it,
I know I can achieve it!
—Reverend Jesse Jackson

SAINTE-REGINA PRIVATE HIGH SCHOOL

Once in Bonneville, the capital city, Onkere's sister Mariella decided to pay for his studies. He was accepted in twelfth grade in a private high school by the name of Sainte-Regina, located in downtown Bonneville not far from the national stadium. Given that Mariella had just been recruited into Mpugu's armed forces and was getting trained, she was receiving a sort of stipend to help her cope with the military reality and pay off her own bills.

Her brother Onkere had to promise her that he would not let her down because she had volunteered to pay for his studies that would cost her, on a monthly basis, almost $200. To pay her back, he promised to do two things. One, he would take care of her house by cleaning, cooking, ironing clothes, and grocery shopping. In short, making sure that the place was radiant and worth living in. Two, he had to graduate. Not only did Onkere really know what he wanted, but he also knew what was required to achieve that objective.

The protagonist knew that twelfth grade was the last grade in which graduation would wildly open doors to any university worldwide. Thus, the time had come for him to unequivocally move to that next level up by graduating. He furthermore knew that graduation required certain self-discipline, not self-indulgence. He had no margin of error whatsoever. The opportunity offered by his sister was his last shot, and he had to get it right. For that to happen, he had to be more focused than ever before.

He also had to graduate to prove wrong those who wanted him held back to eleventh grade, by showing them that he had what it took to be in twelfth grade. But he, above all, wanted to graduate the same time as would his friends and classmates back in Toshville. Onkere and I also knew perfectly that once they graduated, they all would unquestionably pursue university studies. As a matter of fact, Onkere, Dylan, and I had more than once discussed this issue. We all, therefore, knew that we would be attending the English department upon graduating. Understandably so, nobody, let alone Onkere, wanted to miss that rendezvous with destiny, so to speak.

Forester was one of the advanced students who were excellent at English. While Richy and the protagonist were seventh graders at O&R Private High School back in Toshville, Forester attended the English Club under their leadership. He was an active member of the club who contributed to its success by bringing great ideas and sometimes documents that would allow debates or discussions. Dylan and Onkere knew him from a long time ago. Forester, Dylan, Richy, and the protagonist became all friends. Their love for the English language brought them very close over the years.

I cannot recall, however, whether Forester actually attended the big show Richy and Onkere put together with the English Club while the protagonist was still attending O&R Private High School back in Toshville. Forester seemed to be more mature than Onkere. As such, he was more reserved. One could tell that he was well mannered and knew how to carry himself around ladies. He liked to dress nice while looking good. Forester was very bright and stubborn. He was a true gentleman who adored pet animals and exotic sceneries. He disliked the smell of any sort of alcoholic beverage that some students engaged in during breaks.

While attending Sainte-Regina Private High School, Onkere had a clear objective: do whatever it takes to graduate. He had already long ago made an assessment of his academic weaknesses and strengths. He knew perfectly well that in order to graduate, for example, he needed to maintain a two-and-a-half score in mathematics and aim as high as he could in the humanities-related subjects. Therefore, he would work harder in all subjects but English, where, truth be told, he had acquired enough knowledge, sufficiently surpassing the minimum required for a twelfth grader.

Throughout the year, he had his eyes open and worked toward scoring high in any subject presented to him. He made sure to be on time in all his classes. He actually attended all of them. He took notes during all the classes. He also asked questions to get clarification whenever necessary. He did pretty well in all subjects. He did the assignments and turned them in on time. Onkere became more curious and would always get in touch with his counterparts who were attending public high schools just to be aware of the kind of topics likely to constitute the basis of the national baccalaureate examination.

Onkere's English instructor that year was great. But he did not have much to learn from him because—as already pointed out—everything he was teaching, Onkere had already learned a long time ago. At the time the events being narrated occurred, he already knew more than the basic grammatical English rules.

He had already learned and covered more than four hundred English regular and irregular verbs, and he easily was able to conjugate in the present, past, present perfect, future, and conditional tenses. He furthermore had built an incredible vocabulary, far superior to that of the average twelfth grader. He pretty much knew every vocabulary word dealing with animals, flowers, automobiles, the human body, weather, birds, culinary art, flora, fauna, geography, and locations to name a few. Onkere had by this time methodically mastered the English sentence structure. He also could detect even the slightest nuances in phrasal verbs and prepositions.

Thanks to the Joneses and Ms. Ballwalter, the main protagonist was familiar with using some idiomatic expressions and had no problem understanding or recognizing them within sentences and texts. Truth be told, he had also worked hard at trying to maintaining a certain American way of speaking. In short, there clearly was nothing English related he could learn as a twelfth grader that he did not already know at this point.

As weird as this might sound, because he had almost covered the topic being taught, he did not establish a close relationship with his twelfth-grade English instructor. And that was all right with Onkere because he no longer needed to prove to any instructor what he was capable of or try to befriend any instructor for that matter. All he wanted was to focus more on the rest of the subjects where he knew he had weaknesses and try to resolve them before the national baccalaureate started.

Looking back at reasons why he failed to bond with the instructor, I think it was due to the fact that Onkere had a far more advanced level and grasp of the English language compared to the rest of his classmates. Arguably, from a general standpoint, the majority of the students who were attending most of the private high schools fell into two categories. The first one would be students who had been expelled from other high schools because they performed poorly, thus revealing some sort of weaknesses in many subjects. The second category was usually associated with students who, for some reason, had dropped out for years and were returning to school.

Given these reasons, those students were now considered as having special needs. The instructor needed to be soft and go slowly on the subject being taught. And in the case under analysis, the instructor was teaching English. Unfortunately for our main protagonist, he did not fall into either category. He fell into the group of students not liking mathematics, but he had tremendous abilities in the rest of the topics being taught at high school levels.

Onkere's accurate command of the English language made his instructor respect him. He would sometimes authorize Onkere to teach the class some afternoons on his behalf, especially if he knew he would be late.

As more days passed, Onkere focused on his studies. All he did was study, go to school, return home and read, eat, and go to bed to repeat the routine the next day. Over and over and over again. Over some weekends, he would clean his sister's house or do the dishes for her. While at his sister's house, Onkere had to share a bedroom with his nephew for about nine months. During those months, he refused to attend any public pub or event. All he did was read and study lessons he did not understand. Again, he even worked harder at maintaining a two-and-a-half score in mathematics. Onkere worked rather hard on French and French literature. He improved his knowledge of Spanish, history, geography, and philosophy. In all of these subjects, he made sure that he would not score below twelve out of twenty during the national baccalaureate examination. He spent more than five to eight hours per day studying for the national baccalaureate, his ultimate goal.

THE NATIONAL BACCALAUREATE

Two semesters into the school year, Onkere had to test the theory that he could graduate and obtain the baccalaureate by maintaining a two-and-a-half score in math during the national examination, while scoring high in the rest of the subjects. The Francophone grading system is based on the French one, which is based on a twenty-point scale. At high school, the passing grade is ten, which is average. In order to get to that passing grade, all the final grades obtained from the various subjects are put together and then divided into the corresponding number of subjects. Grades are compensatory to one another. What this means is that a student could still have a two and a half out of twenty in one subject and still pass with flying colors if the said student has scored excellent grades in the rest of the subjects. Thus, one failed score in one particular subject only—math, for the protagonist—does not necessarily predict failure at the end of the semester or a national examination.

Like all high schools, Sainte-Regina held its prebaccalaureate examination, and Onkere passed it with flying colors. While he scored the failing grade of two and a half out of twenty in mathematics, he nonetheless received excellent grades in the rest of the subjects, allowing for compensation of the failing grade he got. He notably received sixteen out of twenty in English.

He probably scored about thirteen out of twenty in Spanish, given that he was as good at that foreign language. I do not remember the exact scores in the rest of the subjects. Still, I am positive he scored as high as he could in the rest of the topics, part of the preexamination.

Coming successfully out of the preexamination, Onkere was more confident and aware of what needed to be done. He knew that he had to repeat and maintain the scores he got during the preexamination his high school just organized to get the baccalaureate and pass the subsequent national examination, during which all twelfth graders compete in order to graduate. That moment, when it comes, brings a lot of stress and sometimes panic. Students, therefore, need to be focused to avoid getting distracted.

The baccalaureate examination is considered a big deal for twelfth graders because it is the only real moment they have to test everything they have acquired and learned throughout the school year. It also could be perceived, rightly so, as the unique moment twelfth graders actually experiment with what they have learned, going back from primary school all the way up to high school. The baccalaureate is a national examination. As such, it is carried out by the Board of Education, which has the authority to pick and assemble texts, topics, and subjects to be examined by the students. This national examination is carried out simultaneously throughout the country. Given that Mpugu has fourteen provinces, there would be fourteen primary centers where the examination would be administered. Most likely, these primary centers are located in the capital city of each province. There are also secondary centers where the same examination is carried out.

As for the examination itself, it consists of an analysis of a text, topic, or concept picked by the examination committee, which is normally made up of teachers and educators.

In order to ensure its credibility, the Board of Education normally switch instructors from their original high schools and send them to go supervise and administer the examination to other high schools, outside of their comfort zones. As such, the examination can sometimes become a weird moment for some students. In fact, because part of the examination could be carried out in locations students are familiar with, it could be administrated by instructors unfamiliar to particular students. All the ingredients are there that could potentially distract students and contribute to their failure: new settings, new faces, new instructors supervising how the examination is carried out, or separations of classmates into different classrooms.

The examination itself is also made up of three parts. First, students have a sports-related examination, which can be performed either physically or in writing. Then comes the written part of all the subjects. This part is followed by the oral part of the examination. There are two rounds associated with the examination. During the first round, the students who get the grade point average of ten out of twenty graduate, whereas those who get close to that grade point average are given a second chance to go again over the exam. It can be done either orally or, once again, in writing. The students have to choose which way to go.

Needless to say, Onkere, Dylan, Forester, and I knew all about the way the baccalaureate examination was carried out and the kind of pressure that could be put upon twelfth graders, before, during, and after taking it. We needed to be really focused. This explains maybe why Onkere did not want any distraction, even though he had a friend who happened to be a female. Given that both of them were twelfth graders attending the same private high school, they would study together, trying to help each other.

Rebecca, to speak of her, was very good at math, and Onkere needed guidance from someone who could encourage him to work even harder on that topic. As for him, Onkere volunteered to work with Rebecca on three of his favorite subjects. It was kind of natural that the two appreciated each other's studying company. Like Onkere, Rebecca was brilliant and determined to graduate. Rebecca was a remarkable individual with a very unique taste in culinary art. She was a bright, affectionate, soft person who knew what she wanted in life. She was taller than the majority of her friends. She was an idealistic person who saw the world as a wonderful place to live in. She loved eating sandwiches during breaks. Originally from the Midwest of Mpugu, she was of a darker skin color. She had short, ebony-black, thin hair that she apparently had no problem combing each morning prior to rushing off to school.

I cannot say that while Onkere was attending Sainte-Regina Private High School, he encountered any challenger in his English class as he had previously. There certainly was a young man, whose name I think was Freddy. He was smart and good at English. Yet Onkere had reached such a level that no student could surpass him. I need to say that the protagonist, Rebecca, Freddy, and his sister who was also in our class ended up all being friends. We would sometimes work together. Most of the time, we had in mind the same objective: getting the baccalaureate and moving to universities. Freddy was a bit taller than Onkere. He spoke calmly with confidence. He was bright and had something to say on any subject brought to his attention. It was a great pleasure to be around him.

As days and months passed, the national examination was getting closer, to the extent that before we knew it, the time had come to actually sit for it. At the time the events being described occurred, I had already moved to the capital city, about the same time Onkere did. I, as well, had been attending, for some reason and even without knowing it, Sainte-Regina Private High School, the same private high school Onkere was attending. So, I found myself sitting for the same national baccalaureate examination Dylan, Forester, Onkere, Rebecca, Freddy, his sister, and the rest of Mpugu's twelfth graders were about to take.

THE EXAMINATION

On the eve of the examination, however, I pretty much did not sleep. I think I was very stressed out. Understandably so. Many things were going through my mind.

One thing that I did not do—for which I am proud till this day—was glance at any of my school documents or notes. I did not revisit any lesson. Instead, I listened to some of my favorite musical masterpieces by Dolly Parton, Don Williams, Kenny Rogers, John Denver, Phil Collins, Tracy Chapman, Bob Marley, Edie Brickell, and Sam Cooke. By then, I had also come to appreciate a song by Scott McKenzie entitled "If You're Going to San Francisco." Jim Croce's "I'll Have to Say I love You in a Song" had also been one of my favorite songs. Listening to music during such an important moment in my life was my way of releasing some of the pressure that had been building up the past months. To be honest, I heard from Rebecca, Onkere, Freddy, and his sister pretty much the same story, though slightly different in terms of the tool used to release the pressure.

Of all my friends, Onkere was the only one effectively using music as a therapeutic way of releasing stress. As for Rebecca, she felt sick. Freddy spent his time jogging and walking by the beach, while his sister, whose name I have now forgotten, spent time reading religious books.

The morning of the first day of the examination, I was more than ready to get the ball rolling. So was Onkere. He, as a matter of fact, had been stressing out and wanted to be done with the examination. Given that he actually did not like practicing sports at a high level, he had to analyze, in writing, a sporting event. Later that day, he was very confident about his performance. The following day, things got more serious because the written part of the examination started on that day. Again, at the end of the day, he felt very optimistic about his performance. The written part of the examination lasted for about three to four days. The last part, which consisted of speaking foreign languages, was the most interesting part for him. As a matter of fact, upon hearing his name, Onkere, who had been preparing all his texts, handed them to the examiner, a medium-sized black man speaking English with a good accent. One could tell that he was very confident in expressing himself. Upon receiving the texts handed to him, the instructor picked one out of them. The subsequent discussion that unfolded was based on that text. Right away, the instructor was friendly and joked a bit to make Onkere get comfortable. Then he proceeded to ask him to read the text, which he did. Less than two minutes into reading the text, Onkere was abruptly stopped by the instructor, who asked him the following questions: "Have you recently been in an English-speaking country? Or have you lived in an English-speaking country?"

"No, sir. I haven't," answered the young examinee from Akaga City.

One could clearly notice that the examiner did not believe him, considering the way he read the text and also how fluent, confident, and comfortable he was. Most importantly, the instructor's suspicions were due to the fact that he was amazingly and unexpectedly impressed by the way the examinee was sounding and pronouncing words and entire sentences while reading the text. Seeing that Onkere was really making no effort whatsoever expressing himself in such a relaxed manner, the instructor dropped his line of questioning, which was supposed to be based on the picked text. Then both the examiner and the examinee went toe-to-toe, branching out, discussing his main objectives upon receiving the baccalaureate degree, which the instructor already anticipated he would get, precisely because of the impressive way the discussion had been carried out from the examinee's end. The examiner even strongly recommended that he enroll in the English department of Bonneville University upon receiving his degree.

I remember the examiner almost begging the examinee to attend the English department, arguing that it would be such a loss and waste of an added value if he chose to enroll in a different department.

At the end of the examination, the examinee had the feeling that things went well. He nailed it and believed that things could not have been better.

At the end of the entire examination, we all had to wait for the results to come in. The waiting moment was a killer. Morally, physically, and spiritually, most students are generally worn out after the whole examination. So was Onkere. Finally, less than two weeks after the examination, the results came in. We all rushed to the examination center. Onkere, Freddy, and I passed, while things did not go so well for some of our classmates. It was a moment of bittersweet, mixed feelings that naturally and humanly prevented us from expressing our real joy right there, on the spot. Nevertheless, once we parted ways and Onkere was by himself, returning home to announce the good news to his sister Mariella, he felt a strange feeling. He indeed felt as if he was not touching or hitting the ground while walking. Rather, he felt as though he was literally flying while walking. As for me, I strongly believe that feeling had everything to do with him being not only overjoyed but also overwhelmed from not believing what he had just accomplished, considering all the twists and turns he went through in high school.

Less than sixty minutes after the good news came in, Mister, his wife, and the rest of the Monray family were informed as well.

Days later, when transcripts were released, it showed Onkere nailed it in English. The examiner had rewarded him with a score of eighteen out of twenty—corresponding to A+ in the American grading system—confirming what he already knew. In fact, before getting out of the English examination room, the instructor had told him that he could have scored twenty out of twenty.

Given that the examiner suspected he had lived or at least visited an English-speaking country—hence him being fluent and performing as he did—he would score eighteen out of twenty. However, everyone who knew Onkere's family background could testify that he had never been abroad and had never lived in or visited any English-speaking country.

No member of his family could have afforded to support such a financial burden. Now, that been said, it needs pointing out that the score received by Onkere—eighteen out of twenty—was among the highest, if not the highest received on the national level. As far as I can remember, none of his challengers scored higher than eighteen out of twenty. This could be proof that on a national capacity, the examinee was among the best students in English. Strangely enough, as he had anticipated, he scored two and a half out of twenty in math. Yet because of the compensatory system, regardless of that failing grade, he still obtained his baccalaureate degree with flying colors. The news of Onkere getting the baccalaureate degree spread like wildfire throughout the country. At the same time, he learned and read out of the national journal that Dylan and Forester had also brilliantly succeeded in obtaining the same degree. This meant that they would be attending the English department at Bonneville University as well. That national university was the only one all of them could afford, given that it was a public university. And that was also the only university attended by the majority of students from low-income families. That being said, I can only imagine that like myself, Onkere, Dylan, and Forester were probably also eager to be enrolled in the English department.

Normally, twelfth-grade graduation is supposed to be followed by a big party organized by the family of the graduates. As for Onkere and I, no party was thrown for us. Onkere's sister Mariella could not throw a party for him because she had been paying for his studies throughout the year. Meanwhile, Onkere and I had to be content with attending parties thrown for our mutual friends or other students from our high school. It was great to meet with friends and classmates and talk about all the tireless moments we spent studying for the examination. We also knew that after the parties, many of us would go our separate ways. While some might go overseas, others would be attending national universities. Months following Freddy's party, I learned that his sister and he had gone to South Africa to pursue their studies. As for Onkere and I, we got ready to attend Bonneville University, the only one we could afford. Yet, like Onkere, I wished I could have gone to South Africa, France, or even the United States to pursue my studies. Unfortunately, nobody within our respective families had enough money to support us. Onkere, nevertheless, was comfortable attending Bonneville University. The truth is that upon being conferred the baccalaureate degree, Onkere and one of his cousins named Erst could have been offered a scholarship to attend any university of their choice overseas. Their distant cousin, whose name I no longer remember, who could have done such a great and honorable, positive action, flatly turned them down. That kind of selfish behavior was, unfortunately, an occurrence from that distant cousin of theirs.

CHAPTER 5

Bonneville University: English Department

Education is the passport to the future, for tomorrow
belongs to those who prepare for it today.
—Malcolm X

LIFE ON CAMPUS

As the months were getting closer to the next academic
year, Onkere knew that some major changes were going to
happen. One of these changes had to do with him leaving
his sister's home and finding a place of his own. He had now
earned the independence to live by himself. With the help of
Mariella, they did what they could to find him a room on
campus so he could stay close to the university. He liked that
idea very much. Life in the dormitory was exciting but also
challenging. College students were put by pairs of two in one
small bedroom. Roommates were randomly picked despite
the process established for assigning rooms. This means that

they were strangers who had to get on well with each other. They had to accommodate each other accordingly. In some cases, some students would bring furniture, television sets, microwaves, or a fridge on move-in days. Onkere had no problem fitting in. As soon as he got the room, he quickly enjoyed his new life on campus. The dormitory, to speak of it, was made up of six buildings, one of which an alphabetic letter had been assigned to. As for Onkere, he was assigned to building D.

Life on campus was exciting because we got the opportunity to meet many college students from all around the country, as well as some foreign ones from other parts of Africa. The campus was a place where university students would engage in debates, sometimes passionately and occasionally violently. A lot of partisan politics were also part of the atmosphere.

The students not sharing the political views of the people in power would openly disagree, making their views known to the entire university community. It was awesome. Once in a while, it was scary. It was always intellectually challenging.

THE FRESHMAN YEAR

At the beginning of the fall semester, as it turned out, Dylan, Forester, Onkere, and I found ourselves enrolled in the English department of Bonneville University. We were so excited because, as I have been arguing, it was a relief to all of us to know that we would now only deal with humanities topics.

Dylan, Forester, Onkere, and I reconnected quickly. We understood right away that we needed to focus in order to move up to the next level. Furthermore, we were glad because we already knew that all the topics we would be discussing or learning would be carried out solely in the English language. Now freshmen, Onkere and his friends were going to learn certain topics, such as English grammar or translation. They would also learn American literature and civilization, English literature and civilization, and African literature and civilization. Additionally, there would be courses on listening, transcription, phonetics, and applied English.

Onkere was more than jubilant because now he would practice and improve his hearing abilities as well as speaking and writing skills. The freshman year was going to determine the rest of the years to come. In fact, a lot of students are enrolled during that first year. Unfortunately, few out of them graduate up to the next level. And those who move past the freshman year are likely to succeed and ultimately graduate from the department.

The freshman year is indicative of what a funnel system is all about. It is the year of selectivity, whereby only a few best students are rewarded by moving up to the next level, while the majority of students are held back. In the long run, those students just drop out or switch departments.

Coming originally from the Haute-Savana province, Dylan, Forester, Onkere, and I knew that we had to perform excellently well in order to graduate and move up to the next level. Our place of origin had created a solid bond among us. We also knew we had to do whatever it took to help one another succeed. In fact, at the university level, like in all the departments, the intellectual competition was no longer between Forester, Dylan, Onkere, and me, who came from the same province. Instead, it was now a disguised sort of competition between us and them—the others. This trend or way of doing business had unfortunately been going on in academia for years before we even got there. The concealed competition was not just tribe based, but it also was ethnic and occasionally regional related. The majority of the professors were aware of this sad reality. They kept this practice going. Some of them applied subjective considerations as well as partisan politics as a way to punish some college students while rewarding others. By the time these events occurred, there was pretty much, in the English department, only one professor from the Haute-Savana province.

The first year at the university was weird. Things were a bit different. Students were much older. Therefore, there seemed to be no assistance whatsoever offered to them while in class. The instructors would come and make lessons without really giving them much explanation. It would be up to the students themselves to figure things out on their own. One easily understands that things could have been tricky even for excellent students like Forester, Dylan, Onkere, and myself. A young girl by the name of Ashley had joined our group in the meantime. Ashley was a very lovable young lady who knew what she wanted in life. She was very eager to learn new ideas and try to materialize them into action. She was a pragmatic student. She was of a dark complexion, like her friend Onkere. She had long, curvy hair that went to her shoulder. She also had a joyful personality that shined upon people around her whenever she cracked a joke. All of her friends appreciated the uniqueness of the sound of her laugh. She was adorable.

Even though she was from the third most important province of Mpugu, we all nevertheless welcomed her. We all knew that we needed to get focused. Given the scope of the university, the English department, and the number of students attending it, distraction was not part of our English vocabulary. There were about four to five hundred freshmen attending the department. So, Forester, Ashley, Dylan, Onkere, and I had to successfully emerge triumphant out of this mass of students. We pretty much liked all our instructors. Out of all the courses we took, I liked grammar, literature, and civilization classes.

As it turned out, I had very good listening skills and did not have problems with phonetics. Many freshmen experienced difficulties transcribing expressions out of the numerous texts we worked on throughout the academic year. Onkere shared with me that he did not have the kinds of issues those students were having. One of the reasons lots of students had tremendous difficulties with phonetics was partly due, in all fairness, to the fact that the professor teaching that subject was not an expert in the field. She did not hold a degree in that area. In fact, she was more into the agricultural sector. She was more like a business type of woman.

Many students did not like her style. I certainly did not like her teaching style. I believe Onkere, with whom I talked about this issue, did not like her style either. I do not remember how Dylan, Forester, or Ashley felt about this particular course. Onkere liked the grammar instructor. She was a nice lady who could make the less intelligent student in her class understand the lesson being taught. She would encourage all students, Onkere included, to seek explanations in case they did not get the lesson. She had a maternal instinct that naturally allowed her to help students. Additionally, she did everything she could not to fail students on purpose, unlike some of her colleagues.

Of all the topics in the English department's curriculum, Onkere, as could be expected of him, most appreciated American literature and civilization. In fact, two to three months into attending different classes and taking different lessons from different professors, he and his classmates' part of their group—Dylan, Forester, and Ashley—had already chosen what each of them would specialize in. Dylan and Forester picked African literature and civilization. Both of them felt they knew much more about African literature and civilization because that topic, even though taught in English, dealt with literature and civilization of African countries. They strongly felt they needed to know much more about Africa and African history. As for Ashley, she was not so sure what to pick.

Even though she ended up picking British literature and civilization, we could tell that down the road, she still could switch her major. As for Onkere, he picked, for obvious reasons, American literature and civilization. Those were the only three areas any student from our department could specialize in. As for me, I picked British literature and civilization.

Once our choices were made, all we needed to do was to make sure that each and every one of us did what was needed to be done so we could be the best. Remember: we no longer were competing among us. We were now competing against them, the other excellent students from other regions of the country. We felt, consciously or unconsciously, that we had, figuratively speaking, to take the fight to them, which all five of us did.

At the university level, one's knowledge of the English language is judged by one's capacity to correctly write, understand, and fluently speak the language. At the end of the day, one would ultimately graduate based on the scores one obtains. Onkere, as well as his squad members, intended on doing all the above. In fact, all of them could correctly write, understand, and comfortably speak English. All they had to do was put their skills into action and get the ball rolling once more. This time, however, the process was not going to be easy. For one, we were interacting with roughly five hundred freshmen attending classes. In order to reduce the number of students in classes, it had been decided to place them into four or five groups made up of one hundred students. Still, it was hard to play one's cards right. Additionally, the freshmen who had been held back the previous year would do whatever they could to derail new freshmen's chances to graduate and move up to the next level. All things considered, the odds really seemed to be against new freshmen.

It was in such an atmosphere that Onkere and his squad members did all they could to successfully graduate and move up to the next level. They spent countless hours studying and working toward perfecting themselves. Onkere worked harder in American literature and civilization. He did everything he possibly could to be in an excellent standing academically speaking. He made sure that he never failed in that subject, which he did not. During this time, he learned about the history of America, notably how the United States came to be the superpower it is today.

In his American course, he also learned about the American war against Great Britain, the thirteen colonies, the Civil war, American slavery, and the American government and its three branches, legislative, executive, judiciary. He also learned about the system of checks and balances and much more. It was during his freshman year that he learned a lot about the civil rights movement and one of its charismatic leaders, Dr. Martin Luther King Jr., whom, at this point, he already was familiar with. He also learned about the nationalism ideology associated with Malik-El Shabazz, known as Malcolm X. By the time producer and director Spike Lee's movie about Shabazz came out in 1992, Onkere, who had read Alex Haley's 1965 autobiography of Malcolm X, had already grasped what needed to be known about Malcolm X, the Nation of Islam, and the ideology associated with the religion of Islam.

Given that the majority of the assignments were research-based work, most of the grades were, therefore, based on oral presentations in front of the entire class. Freshmen were required to come to class and present their findings on topics assigned to them. Onkere enjoyed those moments because he was fluent in English. He, more than the majority of freshmen, felt confident and comfortable expressing himself in English. Truth be told, Dylan, Forester, and Ashley also enjoyed speaking in front of the class because they too were fluent and felt comfortable orally expressing themselves.

There were some other students who were as confident as Onkere, Dylan, Forester, and Ashley. Among the students taking the intellectual fight to our squad was a certain young, nice-looking man. He was very talkative. He really was excellent at English and had fun expressing himself. Talking was like one of his favorite sports. Because he enjoyed showing off while practicing that sport, many of us thought that he was a womanizer of some sort. In fact, female classmates were always around him. I did not appreciate his sarcasm at all.

Onkere and his squad members did oral presentations in all the subjects that are part of the English curriculum, except for grammar, translation, and phonetics. As already stated, Onkere and his squad members worked hard as freshmen. They established themselves as a force that could be counted on within the English department. They ended up being recognized by some sophomore, junior, and even senior students.

Fefe, the person who literally introduced the English language to Onkere, had been attending the same English department for over three years. He was a junior who had already been conferred an associate's degree and was working toward the bachelor's one. It was appropriate, if not natural, that Onkere got back to him, seeking some information about how the department worked and what was expected out of its students. Apart from Fefe, there was another student by the name of Garry, a friend of Randy, Onkere's brother. He was a senior. Onkere and his squad members would sometimes seek help from him too, given that he, as well, was from the Haute-Savana province. As already indicated, at the university level, bonds among students are seriously reinforced if they come from the same province, region, city, or neighborhood.

At the end of their freshman year, Onkere, Dylan, Forester, and I graduated. But we also had mixed emotions and feelings. Realizing all the odds that we overcame, we wanted to enjoy ourselves for having succeeded. Graduating meant a lot to Onkere, who had been seriously focusing on school. Upon graduating, he decided to take a break when summer came. He traveled back to Toshville to spend some quality time with his parents and the rest of the family.

THE MOTHER-SON SPECIAL BOND

Once back to Toshville, he reconnected with Richy and Ziguy. The reason I stopped talking about Richy until now is that when Onkere left Toshville for Bonneville, the capital, to continue twelfth grade, he kind of lost touch with both of his friends. The first had by now found great job opportunities. I appreciated the fact that he was having a great time doing the type of job he was doing when we all reconnected. As for Ziguy, as it turned out, he too had found employment, and was enjoying himself. He was about to create a family of his own, I was told. I could not have been happier for him.

On top of those new realities, Onkere was more than grateful to get back to his roots. He was also blissfully happy because, since graduating from high school two years ago, he had not seen his parents. His mother, whom he had been missing, had been asking about him. So, it was great to see the two of them reunite.

There is a family story known only by the Monray family members, according to which his mother and he had a special bond. Mrs. Monray told the story herself to her children, which is that while being pregnant with Onkere, his mother experienced no health-related issue or any other uncomfortable moment women ultimately go through during pregnancies. Rather, Mrs. Tassina Monray felt great and energetic. She graciously would tell her children that she enjoyed being pregnant with Onkere.

I believe Onkere's middle child ranking or position has certainly something to do with it. Because the main protagonist had been told this story, he would brag about being his mother's adored child. He obviously enjoyed being around his mother.

One could tell that the feeling was mutual. Saying this on my part does not necessarily mean that Onkere was the preferred child, or that his mother loved him more than she loved his siblings. Only a parent would know that. Mrs. Tassina Monray never said anything about loving him more than any of his sisters or brothers. Never. Ever. What I am saying here is that parents, according to certain situations or events, can love their children accordingly. Equally, certainly. In different ways maybe, even though they would never say so.

One situation happened in Onkere's life where his mother stepped up to the plate to protect him from harm, or so she thought. In fact, because of employment opportunity, Mister's first place of employment was actually Bonneville, where the main protagonist attended primary school for about a year before the whole family returned to Toshville. The story goes that on his first day of school, Onkere was so distressed, lost, and scared that he spent about two hours crying, rolling over the ground, and disturbing the class quietness. Unable to control him and contain his irritability, the decision was made to summon his parents to go get him. Naturally, as could have been expected, Mister showed up.

Upon seeing his father, Onkere, who was still crying, all shook up, gradually contained himself. One could clearly perceive a sense of relief on the boy's beaming face.

Upon learning about the trouble her son had gone through, once the latter got back home, his mother comforted, bathed, clothed, and affectionately fed him. All was done in that order. She was almost opposed to sending him back to school the next day. But Mister did not want to hear any emotional outburst based on feelings rather than reason—I am the one being specific here. A conversation inevitably ensued between the couple. Following the discussion, his mother let him attend school the next day.

In the meantime, she and her husband made sure their son was switched to the class being attended by one of his neighborhood friends. Because of this event, while growing up, Mister would always remind our protagonist that he once hated school and that, as a consequence, he had no lesson to give his younger brother Tom. In Onkere's case, however, the reality is that there was no familiarity recognizable in any of the faces in his class. Additionally, he was very young, about three or four years old. The attitude exemplified by Mrs. Tassina Monray, however, was said to be indicative of her special love and bond to her son.

At the time this event occurred, Onkere was the youngest child, whereas Yogi was still a baby. Eyila was the oldest member of the family, followed by the twin sisters, Mariella and Olivia. Randy was next, followed by the protagonist himself. Djoka was still living in Akaga City, whereas the oldest among the girls, Mariana, a licensed primary school teacher, was living in Toshville. Lino, the protagonist's other brother, a licensed primary school teacher as well, was not in the picture yet. The oldest of the entire family, Lens, also known by his nickname Indien, had left the family household a long time ago. Lens Indien was a tall black man with a cheerful personality. He had very short, brown, thick hair and a small, flat nose. He smiled rarely but would once he had accomplished some impossible task to be accomplished by average people. He was a fast thinker who could read voluminous books in days.

Back in the early seventies, he had gone to look for employment opportunities in the third largest province of Mpugu, in terms of population. Lens Indien was exceedingly brilliant and was the first among Onkere's family members to attend high school. In the late sixties, he was encouraged by Mister and Mrs. Monray, his parents, to look for job opportunities booming all over Mpugu in the early seventies. I remember him coming to visit the Monray family in Bonneville during summers. During those times, he was the only family member possessing a camera. He took pictures of his siblings that became important memory material, allowing me to narrate the story. Big brother Lens Indien enjoyed photography, traveling, and traditional music by national singers of those days. He was funny when he wanted to be and tough on his little brothers and sisters when he needed to be, as well. But most of the time, he was nice and generous to his siblings.

I remember one day he traveled from Niceville, the capital city of the third largest province of Mpugu, to Toshville. He made a stop, visiting his parents and siblings living in Bonneville. During that specific stop, he distributed large amounts of cash to all his siblings. I remember seeing Onkere being agitated because he got three or four large bills whose value, at that time, he did not know. In fact, Onkere was about four years old.

As for the stories about the middle child, especially regarding Onkere's ranking and position within the Monray family, they differ from one culture to another. Plus, they can be either positive or negative ones. For example, in some African cultures, middle children are thought to possess some sort of extraordinary capacities regarding the anticipation of events, good as well as bad. Middle children also have more freedom than firstborn ones. Parents are likely to have high expectations for their firstborn, which could potentially constitute a source of the pressure cooker for children finding themselves in that position. In the meantime, middle children could take a free ride. Personally, I saw this kind of situation within the Monray family. The father, Mister, had placed this kind of pressure on his son Randy. In fact, Mister made sure that Randy succeeded in school because he eagerly wanted his son to be successful in life. Onkere witnessed quarrels occurring between Mister and Randy almost constantly whenever the latter was not doing what their father expected out of him. Onkere furthermore witnessed passionate misunderstandings between Mister and Mariella or Mister and Olivia because their father wanted them to succeed in their lives as well.

From Mister's point of view, education was the only true key for his children to become successful. This means that he stressed the importance of receiving an education to all his children. He did what he could to make his point clear. As for Onkere, I don't remember seeing him having misunderstandings with his parents. He was so smart that he would not dare challenge his dad's decisions.

That being said, once back among his family members, Onkere appreciated being around his sisters, nieces, nephews, and cousins. He was most likely cheerful to see his younger brother Tom, who had been born a long time ago. Tom was almost a teenager by now. Being Mister's last son, Tom, unlike his older brothers, was spoiled in every aspect of his life while growing up. After having been away for two years, Onkere spent much time with his parents and family members instead of hanging out with his friends. He was now a young man who knew what he wanted in life. Whenever Richy or Ziguy wanted to hang out, he would nicely invite them over while explaining that he really was worn out. To avoid hurting his friends' feelings, he almost had to justify himself by telling them that he needed a refill of energy before returning to the university for round two. And because of that, relaxing and tranquility were all he had gone to Toshville for.

Before the summer drew to its end, Onkere had to say goodbye to his beloved parents, siblings, and friends, after which he traveled back to Bonneville.

SOPHOMORE: YEAR 1

The sophomore year was a bit complicated. Onkere had not anticipated what the outcome would be. The squad was now made up of four members: Dylan, Forester, Onkere, and I. Additionally, lessons were a bit advanced, and some of the instructors we had as freshmen no longer had us. We had to adjust to the new ones. As could be expected, new topics were now part of the curriculum. Among them was English linguistics. Onkere liked the instructor. He consequently did the best he could to maintain grades above average even though it was not at all a piece of cake. As the months passed by, Onkere could feel that things were not working out, especially because the majority of the new instructors seemed not to care about students. Some would show up late. Others would send hard copies of documents to be analyzed through one student representative, who would either disappear or ask for the rest of the students to pay to have copies made available to them. He would sometimes overcharge. There was a sort of dysfunctional organization that ultimately derailed Onkere's attention and made it more than hard for him to get on time the necessary documents or information that would help him go through his notes. Most of the time, the student representatives were the ones who had been held back the previous year, and their intentions were to contribute to the failure of new students, to the extent that they would disappear for days if not weeks with the documents or information.

Even though there was still a squad of four members, the truth is that Dylan, Forester, Onkere, and I each wanted, at some point, to be our own individual, thus work on our own. The intent of working on an individual basis was never discussed among the squad members. But I definitely can assert that it was there. Things were also made a bit complicated for Onkere because the group members were now scattered into other groups established by the department's chair, on alphabetical order. Therefore, Dylan and I were separated from Forester, who was also disjoined from Onkere. Additionally, sophomore year coincided with a presidential election. Therefore, Bonneville being Mpugu's capital, some of the main political activities were planned and carried out around campus. Some of those activities were sometimes initiated by students. Politicians would descend onto the campus looking for any student willing to be part of a political party or help as they could with doing the grassroots work. In this regard, Onkere willingly joined his brilliant brother Randy, a fourth-year law school student, to organize a grassroots campaign for candidate Nganstie. The intensity of his political activism and involvement would eventually lead our main protagonist to take his eyes off the ball for a while, not anticipating the consequences related to his academic near future. The political activism came also with traveling from town to town, and from city to city. Given that Onkere is from the Haute-Savana region, he and the rest of the political organizers working on behalf of candidate Nganstie had to travel to Toshville, the political bastion of their candidate, so as to campaign there.

Meanwhile, students attending the university, whose place of origin was the Haute-Savana province, had put together an association called Tari. Its fundamental aim was to defend and protect their socioeconomic, academic, cultural, and political interests within the university framework. Together with Tari's members, Onkere would frequently travel to the Haute-Savana region. It was during one of those trips that he met a brilliant young lady by the name of Coretta. She was from the history department. The two struck up a brief friendship that ended in a mysterious way, just as it started. Needless to say, the combination of all these exogenous factors did not create a prosperous learning environment for the protagonist to academically meet the requirements to graduate. Meanwhile, Dylan, Forester, and I were successfully conferred the associate degree.

The next year, we went on to work toward completing the bachelor's degree. I was delighted for our success while being sad, at the same time, for our mutual friend. More specifically, I was disgusted with the protagonist because he had proven many times that he had what it took to graduate. Instead of blaming himself, Onkere quickly made an assessment of the reasons he was not successful. Failing the sophomore year was, in retrospect, a blessing in disguise for him. The next year, he really revealed his true character and what he was capable of. If there is one positive trait he got from his father, I would argue, it was stubbornness, especially in refusing to give up. As musically inclined as he was, Onkere certainly shared the assertion of a country music legend, that people build on failure and use it as a stepping-stone. That people who have failed should close the door on the past. That they should not try to forget mistakes made or dwell on them. It has been demonstrated that what is important in such a situation is not how many times a person can get knocked down. What matters is, rather, how quickly a person bounces back. In that respect, an American president argued that only those who dare to fail greatly can ever achieve greatly. It is true that Onkere surely spent a very bad summer. Yet all he thought about was returning to the university so as to show what his true character was moving forward.

SOPHOMORE: YEAR 2

The following year, he came back more determined because he had a job to finish. Failure had taught him a great lesson, and he knew that no distraction of any form was allowed. To make the story short, he worked harder and almost dominated in certain topics. He especially did a great job in American literature and civilization, where his scores were among the highest. That year, he came to appreciate the teachings of his applied English professor, who definitely enjoyed having him in his class. A London-trained professor, that instructor enjoyed smoking during breaks. He was knowledgeable, wise, and very articulate. Onkere had tremendous respect for him. Not surprising that the two established a mutual, respectful, professor-student friendship. At the end of the year, because he persevered and did not get discouraged despite his previous failure, Onkere successfully graduated. He was conferred the associate degree and could not have been prouder of himself. The news of him being conferred that degree spread like wildfire to the extent that everyone who knew him was informed.

It goes without saying that his parents and siblings were informed as well. Mister was ecstatic and made it known to everyone who knew him. Retrospectively, the success of Mister's children, not just Onkere, was also, more than to a certain degree, his own success. He considered it a pride to see his children succeed in their respective lives. Onkere's mother was also lighthearted and sparkling, full of joy. And so was every member of his family. As for our main protagonist, graduating meant that he would be working on the bachelor's degree the following fall semester. Sadly enough, in the meantime, a parallel event happened that crushed him and some students from the department. As it turned out, that same year, Fefe, Onkere's mentor and brother-in-law who introduced and inspired him to like

English and ultimately American culture, suddenly went to heaven to sit by the Lord's right hand.

He had been having some health issues that prevented him from staying focused on his studies. The news of his heavenly departure came to all of us, especially Onkere, as a shock. It affected him a great deal. Among the people affected by the sad news was Fefe's roommate by the name of Jay-Jay, whom Onkere knew by socializing with his roommate. Jay-Jay and Onkere also were members of the Tari Association. Jay-Jay was a very nice, soft-spoken person with strong beliefs that he wisely tried to convey during debates amongst peers. Both Jay-Jay and the protagonist would eventually cross paths at the Great Organization in Washington, DC, working on behalf of Mpugu, their country of origin. As for Mariella, by this time, she had already been married for a while. This means that she and Fefe had parted ways over a decade ago. Therefore, she and her brother never discussed his passing.

INVALIDATED ACADEMIC: YEAR 3

The next school year, another unfortunate event occurred. As it turned out, the government of Mpugu declared that academic year an invalidated one. This meant that no student was going to graduate because the university would be shut down.

Therefore, no degree was going to be conferred to anyone. The unexpected news had devastating effects on students' lives. It negatively impacted some students' futures. By this time, Forester had already gone to France to pursue his master's degree. As for Dylan, he was already in the master's program. As for Onkere, this was another setback on the successful path he had been working toward. The whole situation seemed unfair to him. Having choices other than staying at home for an entire academic year, he looked for job opportunities in order to make ends meet. Regardless of him having gotten a stipend for graduating while attending the university, the government suspended it for the duration of the whole invalidated academic year. Having been used to being financially independent, Onkere found a job at a television station operating as a cable company, where he served as assistant to the chief executive officer's assistant. One of the reasons he was successfully hired was because the company was servicing clients from English-speaking countries. Therefore, the CEO wanted to make sure he had some staff members with English abilities of any kind, fluently expressing themselves in that foreign language. It was during that period that, for the first time, Onkere would be paid for doing for the most part what he liked to do—expressing himself in English.

He liked the new position so much so that he even decided he no longer had anything to do with the university. He sincerely thought that he was done, that he had gotten the perfect job. This idea was ultimately motivated by the fact that he thought he was earning good money. In reality, he was making little above $600 on a monthly basis, which he thought was good money. Truth be told, he was still young. Plus, he had neither children nor responsibilities and thought that was the way life went.

It was during this period of time that Onkere met a young, blonde, American lady named Ms. Smith. She had been working as the finance director for the company, even if she was more into the social work field. A strong-willed person, she had very long, soft, thin brown hair that fell down to her slim waist. She had a ladylike personality as well as a bubbly one. She furthermore had a shapely figure with brownish eyebrows. Wearing glasses was an indication of her having eye issues. She was not that complicated when it came to the type of clothes she wore. Ms. Smith pretty much wore stylist clothes whenever necessary. Yet she would not refrain from wearing jeans four days out of seven. She was an outgoing person who focused on planning things in advance. She was more concerned about what tomorrow would be like versus what today is. She was a caring, affectionate, and lovable person with amazing qualities. She was a very bright, quick thinker.

I guess, because Onkere was one of the workers speaking English at the company, that factor helped in them quickly developing a respectful and solid friendship. Given that Ms. Smith was single, as was Onkere at that particular time, the two of them frequently hung out. One day, out of the blue, Onkere asked his colleague if they could go out for a date. She initially turned him down, arguing that the whole idea was unprofessional and thus not appropriate. Yet, through nice and gentle insistence, one day, she ended up giving up. Before both knew it, they were dating. It is my belief that dating Ms. Smith might have contributed to the protagonist not wanting to return to the university and instead continuing to work at the cable company. Yet Onkere's ideas about dropping out of the university would soon be challenged by his brother Randy.

CHALLENGING ONKERE'S LIFE PERSPECTIVES

Fortunately for Onkere, I remember his brother Randy, a third-year doctoral law student working toward successfully completing his dissertation in France, asking him to man up and wake up to face reality. According to Randy, the reality was that his little brother had gone through tough times and had encountered setbacks. Nevertheless, giving up on education, holding only an associate degree in English was not the best way of moving forward. Randy compassionately felt that his little brother would not be willing or able to live a decent life while being financially stable in the future, earning only a little over $600 per month.

In the final analysis, Randy's realistic approach made perfect sense to Onkere, who would have dealt with Mister had he materialized the idea of quitting the university. Following one of the subsequent discussions he had with Randy, he told the latter that he would not return to the university, that if Randy truly believed the realistic approach he pointed out, he had to help him out.

On that note, Randy—I can still remember the conversation till this day—asked his little brother to get in touch with universities in France and bring him a letter of admission received from one of those institutions so he could look for ways to get him a scholarship, ultimately allowing him to continue his studies in Europe as well. Randy—who successfully completed the master's program from Bonneville University in a four-year period, the number of years required for such a targeted degree, which is amazingly remarkable given all the ethnic, tribal, and regional paradigms occurring in the academia—was automatically granted a scholarship to pursue his doctoral program in France. In contrast, given that Onkere had been held back once and was not at the end of his program, he no longer officially met the requirements to be granted any scholarship for overseas studies. He was in a different situation and needed some sort of intervention to be given a scholarship. The situation he found himself in meant that he could get a letter of admission and still might not even get offered a scholarship.

Energized anew by Randy's promise on the one hand, and determined to keep his promise to his brother on the other hand, Onkere wrote to four universities in France, requesting a letter of admission from each of those institutions. Out of those four universities he got in touch with, only one accepted him. Here is the catch: the admission was conditioned upon him accepting being enrolled as a sophomore student.

Putting it another way, he would be admitted on the condition that he would not be accepted in the bachelor's program, which he should have been attending in Bonneville University had the previous year not been declared invalidated. Given that he had grown legitimately tired with the university system back home, wanting to move far away from it regardless of the fact that he would be enrolled as a sophomore, he accepted the offer. Upon receiving the letter of admission, he talked to his immediate boss at the cable company about not renewing his contract and explained to her reasons why not to. He also told his parents that he got a scholarship and was accepted at a university in France. He would be traveling there to pursue his studies. I would be remiss if I omitted a portion of history, which is that upon receiving his admission letter, Randy made sure his brother was going to get a scholarship. He teamed up with a mutual uncle of theirs to find ways to get Onkere a scholarship. Under the pressure made by Randy, their uncle made the magic happen.

By the time he got the scholarship, he had been dating Ms. Smith for about a year, and their relationship had evolved. The two of them seemed to be in love. That is what Ms. Smith told Onkere, and he reciprocated. They spent the remaining time together, prior to Onkere's departure to Europe. On the eve of his departure, he asked his girlfriend whether she would be willing to visit him in France. She answered in a positive way to the request.

CHAPTER 6

Study Abroad: Europe

Nobody can discover the world for somebody else. Only
when we discover it for ourselves does it become common
ground and a common bond and we cease to be alone.
—Wendell Berry

THE TRIP TO FRANCE

Before the departure date and time came, Onkere had to
return to Toshville to say goodbye to his parents. While
his mother was maternally saddened by the departure,
Mister, his father, made it more than clear to him that he
must never abandon his origins and where he came from
no matter what the situation. Mister also argued that his
son was just going to study and had to return home upon
completing his studies. Thus, Onkere committed himself
to returning home upon completing his studies. He put his
father's mind at rest by telling him that he would always
come back to give to the community. Reassured, both of
his parents blessed him and wished him well. That was the

African way. That specific talk between father and son, upon the latter's departure for overseas, had been going on in Africa for centuries. Randy, Onkere's brother, had had the same kind of talk with Mister prior to his departure for France as well. And like his brother, Randy too made the same promise to return home upon completing his studies, which he did.

Upon receiving the blessings from his folks, Onkere traveled to France with one of his little sisters, Opy, who by now had graduated from high school. She was as bright as the rest of the Monray family. She had a bubbly personality that was enjoyed by anyone around her. She was a quick thinker, as were the vast majority of her siblings. And, like most of her sisters, she too was a feminist who dreamed of the idealistic world wherein women and men were given the same rights.

She had gotten a baccalaureate in economics, obtaining subsequently a scholarship to pursue her studies abroad. She had picked France, and Randy, her brother, had gotten her an anticipated letter of admission from the university he was attending.

There they were, Onkere and Opy, about to travel to France, where neither had ever been before. I can only imagine the kind of pressure placed on Onkere, who had to take care of his sister once in Paris. I can remember him telling me that the trip in itself went excellently well. He and his sister were excited and ready for a new adventure. They went through Italy, where they had a one-hour layover. They ate, watched movies, and listened to some music. The trip took them about seven to eight hours. Once in Paris, they were excited to see new faces, buildings, places, and the environment. Wasting time was not allowed because Onkere had first to figure out which train station to drop his sister Opy off at. From Charles de Gaulle Airport, Onkere took her to the north train station that would take her to her final destination, where she was expected by her brother Randy. As for Onkere, once his sister boarded the train, he immediately went to take the one going toward the eastern part of France. During the trip, he spent most of his time looking out the window, contemplating the splendid scenery. He also, from time to time, made sure the train had not passed the station he was supposed to get off at. At other moments, he was suspicious of certain passengers boarding the train. He spent time paying attention to every little move made by people coming in as well as those going out. The trip took about one hour and thirty minutes, if I remember correctly.

REGINA UNIVERSITY

Onkere got to his final destination around one in the afternoon and went straight to the administrative authorities to fill out documents relative to dormitory rules and regulations. Unlike Bonneville University campus where he had to share a room, this time around, he was given a bedroom to himself. Needless to say, he was worn out, and all he wanted to do was to go to sleep even though it was still daytime. He woke up around eight at night, on the same day, wandering around, trying to figure things out. He was also trying to see whether there were students from Mpugu, his country of origin, attending the university and whether they would be on campus. As it turned out, some were, in fact, residing on campus. Amazingly enough, he found one of his old friends from Bonneville University, a young man named Moukoutou. He was attending Regina University even though he was from the department of anthropology. Given that Moukoutou had been living in this eastern part of France for about two years prior to our main protagonist's arrival, he felt the African brotherly obligation to show him around. The next day, Onkere rested because he was worn out still. He and Opy had traveled over the weekend. He had to start school less than two days after his arrival.

SOPHOMORE: 3RD YEAR

The following Monday, the day of school, Onkere, who had already visited the university he would be attending, went straight to the international student registrar to fill out administrative documents.

After, he went to the English department's secretariat, where he was given his class schedule. He then went straight to the first class. He attended four classes on that day. Everything was new to him: professors, students, and class designs. Two of the obvious differences were that, first, all the professors were white men or women. Second, the majority of students were whites as well. It was only then that Onkere realized he was no longer in Africa but Europe.

The first class he attended was called American Autobiography, where famous, historic, and important American heroes from all walks of life were discussed. The course was entirely carried out in American English, I am assuming, by an American professor, if I am not mistaken, by the name of Pitcherson. He was about five feet eight. He liked to wear jeans and never carried any bag on him. Instead, he always carried his books and everything else. Professor Pitcherson had brown, short hair. One thing I personally liked—and I believe Onkere shared my view of this—was the fact that Professor Pitcherson engaged students, always encouraging them to express themselves. This means that not only did the material need to be understood, but students also had to speak and communicate in English with the professor. Thus, a certain efficiency in English was required from students. Onkere liked that dynamic. He logically had already been conferred an associate's degree from Bonneville University. This means that he had already been judged competent for this level. Therefore, he felt he had certain leverage or advantage over the rest of the students, even though the material being covered in this particular course was also new to him. Additionally, he appreciated the fact that some of his classmates shied away from expressing themselves in class. Some would raise their hands, yet, once given the floor, they would get confused or scared.

Others, not many though, more courageous, would express themselves but not to the satisfaction of Professor Pitcherson. To be blunt, they were not public speakers, as was Onkere, who had been perfecting and practicing public speaking through the English Club he once led, together with the many oral presentations magnificently executed while attending Bonneville University. He had gained confidence, a feature his classmates lacked for the most part.

Onkere, whose ability was in not just understanding and writing but also fluently speaking English, had already been proven and recognized with the above-mentioned degree. He seized that opportunity to make it known that he was going to be an incredible student to count on and that Professor Pitcherson had to take him seriously. He was the only black African student attending that class. There was a total of five or six black students attending some of the other courses he was taking. There was basically no difference between the subjects Onkere had studied at Bonneville University and the ones he was now learning. In fact, on top of the American Autobiography course, the other subject being covered was a British civilization class taught by one of the protagonist's favorite British professors by the name of Presley. He was very engaging, open-minded, and acutely aware of Onkere's presence in his class. Professor Presley had darker brown hair, a bit longer than that of Professor Pitcherson. He was understanding, compassionate, and very friendly.

There was a course on American literature taught by an American professor named Martinez. She was a remarkable person with a very unique taste in music and American literature. She was a bright, affectionate, and caring professor. She was as tall as Professor Presley. She loved teaching her course on romanticism. Professor Martinez had brown, short hair and yet, regardless of this, her ladylike type of personality remained intact.

He was also taught by Professor Clara, a French native, a Translation and Interpretation class. Out of all these courses, the latter was the only new addition to the curriculum required for second-year students from Bonneville University. Of all these courses, the first three ones were my favorite, and I guess they were Onkere's as well. I am not sure. Professor Clara was the youngest of all the professors. She was extremely bright and a quick thinker.

She was almost always thinking about something when she was not teaching. She was remarkably beautiful, to the amazement of her students who happened to be male. She dressed nicely à la française—the French way.

Professor Martinez's class was all about analyzing American romanticism's characteristics and some of the poets associated with not only that genre but also the American transcendentalism movement, such as Emerson or Professor Martinez's favorite author, Emily Dickinson. We pretty much studied everything that could possibly be learned about her. As in Professor Pitcherson's class, students were required to demonstrate some efficiency and the ability to orally perform. The majority of the assignments were to be orally presented in front of the entire class. Professor Martinez took time to individually assign topics to her students so as to give them a chance to express themselves. Needless to say, as usual, Onkere could not ask for more. He endorsed this process all the way. It seemed that he was destined to be successful because, in Professor Presley's class, students needed to be good at orally expressing themselves. Efficiency in orality was key. The course on British civilization was a bit new to Onkere. Students had to make the analysis of cartoon documents in order to extract and reveal the relevancy of British historical or important events being described by cartoonists. Students were assigned topics sometimes collectively, but most of the time, they were individually assigned. In both cases, the findings had to individually be orally presented. In all those classes, Onkere dominated, outperforming the rest of the students, the majority of whom were, in all honesty, younger than he was. Rapidly, all three professors—Pitcherson, Presley, and Martinez—noticed that he was excellently performing in their respective classes. All three of them, I am assuming, began to wonder who he was. Individually, they started to get to know him, given that he was always among the students scoring the highest in their classes. Each professor was so impressed with his efficiency and ability to orally express himself that they wanted to know his background and his country of origin considering that this kind of information was private and, therefore, not shared with professors.

As the academic year was drawing to its end, Onkere proved himself to be the best student in terms of scoring the highest in Professor Pitcherson's as well as in Professor Martinez's classes. Even though he was not the best student in Professor Presley's class, he nevertheless was among the best students. He was appreciated by all three professors, whom he had befriended. Upon becoming friends, they started coaching him by revealing how each and every one of them enjoyed having him in their respective classes.

A lot of similarities could easily be established between Mr. Jones and Professor Pitcherson, the latter reminding Onkere of the first mentioned. In fact, both men were white Americans. They pretty much had that same baritone voice and always wore jeans. Both men were tall, very open-minded, and genuinely quick to help students coming from minority groups. Above all, both men, I would argue, were extremely intelligent yet uncommonly humble.

Midway through the first semester, one student who happened to be a French young lady, a bit more mature than the majority of the students, befriended Onkere. Her name was Maldie. She had traveled the world and had lived in Algeria and Great Britain. She had also visited Italy and knew a lot about America. I, like Onkere, was impressed with her knowledge about different places on the planet. She was, understandably enough, as fluent in English as Onkere. She was so friendly that she did everything she could to make him fit in. A strong-willed person, she had very long, soft, thin, dark hair that fell down to her shoulder. She also had a bubbly personality. She was into fashion and took pride in wearing stylish clothes whenever the occasion presented itself. Maldie was an outgoing person who was concerned about the here and now. She was a very pragmatic lady who enjoyed having sandwiches and coffee during our breaks. She appreciated the smell of coffee just like her friend Onkere. She was a caring and lovable person with remarkable qualities. She was a very bright, quick thinker. Being friends with her allowed him to have a better understanding of the French culture as a whole but more specifically that of the eastern region of France. One day, after Professor Pitcherson's class, while waiting for the next one, Maldie suggested that she and Onkere go have a cup of coffee at the university restaurant across the street from the amphitheater. In Onkere's mind, the suggestion sounded like an invitation, and, therefore, he had no objection whatsoever to it.

Also, in his mind, the invite meant that whatever he eventually ordered would be paid for by Maldie, who made the suggestion in the first place.

Mind you that Maldie ordered just a cup of coffee, while Onkere asked for a sandwich on top of the cup of coffee. In the end, when it came time to pay the bill, Maldie only paid for hers and asked Onkere to pay for his. At first, the protagonist did not grasp what was going on for some three or four seconds. And then, suddenly, he told his friend that he had no money on him. Thus, he could not pay for his bill. He then asked Maldie to pay for his, reassuring her that he would pay her money back the next day. The cultural misunderstanding that went down on that day was due to the fact that where Onkere came from, Africa, and precisely Bonneville, the person who invites or suggests that another person goes or accompanies them to a pub or restaurant for a drink, coffee, or dinner is the one who is supposed to pay for the totality of the bill. Based on that cultural reality, Onkere wrongly assumed that Maldie was going to pay for his coffee and sandwich. Maldie, in the meantime, being a French European young lady, assumed that Onkere knew enough about the European culture, which is that, invited or not, whenever people go to the pubs, stores, or restaurants, each individual pays for what they ordered or purchased. Understandably enough, Onkere was culturally shocked when his friend asked him to pay for his portion of the bill. The next morning before class started, Maldie asked her friend about the money he promised to reimburse her. Again, he was still short of money and could not fulfill his promise. Eventually, to settle the matter, the protagonist ended up paying her money back. They ended up being good friends. At the end of the first school year, both Onkere and Maldie graduated. They were successfully conferred associate's degrees—the second one for Onkere—and both moved to the bachelor's program. Like Onkere, for all the reasons that have been explained earlier, I was not that gleefully excited about him being conferred that degree. It was more like a waste of his time because he came to France already holding an associate's degree. But no need to dwell on that aspect of our protagonist's life. When summertime came,

Maldie traveled back to her town to spend the summer with her family. She was not originally from this eastern part of France. Rather, she was from a town located farther south of Regina University, a drive of about forty-five minutes.

By this time of the year, Onkere's girlfriend, Ms. Smith, has already quit working in Bonneville, Mpugu. She had returned to the United States for personal reasons. Onkere tried to convince her to come join him in France. Yet he was unsuccessful. The two of them maintained a steady relationship even if they had been apart for about a year by now. They still were in love with each other, regardless of the fact that the distance was harsh on both of them.

Given that Ms. Smith could not visit the protagonist in Europe, and seeing that he could not travel back to Bonneville because the ticket cost a lot of money, Onkere remained on campus and spent the entire summer in France.

SUMMER ACTIVITIES

What he specifically did during summer instead was, like many of his countrymen, find work on melon plantations. He and his countrymen would work on fields for very long hours during the day through the night. This kind of summer activity was done most of the time just so that they had extra money to keep them afloat while waiting for the stipend money that came late most of the time. The reality is that not everybody could work on those plantations. There was some sort of exploitation going on. The owner, a French lady, knew that the majority of African students did not have sufficient money to finance their studies or live in France. Therefore, they were willing to pretty much do any type of work to get some money, allowing them to pay for bills and survive. Bearing this kind of reality in mind, she made those African and Arab students work like animals, under dire summer weather conditions, unbearable to human beings. Onkere could drive, given that he actually had already passed a driving license test in Mpugu. As an international student, his status allowed him to drive in the French territory with his driving license. Therefore, he volunteered to become his countrymen's personal driver. In that capacity, he drove everybody to work every day. The passengers understood that each of them was supposed to pay him a certain amount of money on a monthly basis.

That money served to maintain the car and take care of extra bills to be paid. The car that was used to transport his countrymen was a white French Renault 5. Six people, Onkere included, were allowed to ride to the plantations. With the money received from working as a chauffeur, he would buy English books, music CDs, and DVDs. He pretty much bought anything he possibly could need in order to become perfect in this language. He purchased *Smallville*'s 2001 series and watched the episodes in its English version to improve his hearing abilities. He furthermore bought English audio books and spent long hours improving his hearing skills, which by now had been quite developed, considering that in his Translation and Interpretation classes, the majority of the activities performed were listening based. In those classes, students spent almost the entire academic year listening and transcribing numerous English topics from audio tapes. To accomplish the assignments, students had headphones on. Even though the assignments proved to be difficult and new at the same time to Onkere, he ended up mastering the process. Back at Bonneville University, there was no language laboratory within the English department. Therefore, students were not trained in this type of exercise. Professor Presley had suggested that Onkere keep working on his diction. He surely had an excellent pronunciation, better than that of the majority of the students. Onkere, in order to improve his way of sounding, purchased lots of books dealing with both English and American sounds and pronunciation.

THE BACHELOR'S DEGREE

When the next school year resumed, Onkere was eagerly motivated to go back because he had had enough time to rest and practice English on his own. Plus, he missed his friends and professors. The new school year was going to be a crucial one. In fact, students attending the bachelor's program were asked to pick what their field of expertise was going to be. Therefore, a professor, who ultimately would be the student's thesis supervisor during the master's program and eventually supervise their doctoral dissertation, needed to be found.

Maldie had no issue picking her field of expertise and finding her master's thesis supervisor. As for Onkere, he definitely had a complicated choice to make between Professors Martinez and Pitcherson, given that he performed excellently well in both of their classes. The truth is that during the previous year, Professor Martinez, following a poetry test where Onkere scored eighteen and a half out of twenty, had had a discussion with him in her office, during which she asked him to pursue the master's degree in American literature. She suggested that if he accepted, she would be more than honored to supervise his master's degree dissertation, upon successfully completing the bachelor's degree he would now be preparing. Meanwhile, Professor Pitcherson had not discussed with him the possibility of supervising his work during the master's degree year. However, he had told Onkere, almost at the end of the previous academic year, that he would do whatever was in his power to make sure he was given an opportunity to go to America under the exchange student program. In fact, Professor Pitcherson, I did not know at the time, was in charge of the exchange program between the university attended by Onkere and some American universities. Of course, upon realizing this news, Onkere shared it with his girlfriend, Ms. Smith. She was overjoyed, as she was probably thinking about the prospect of him residing in America. Ms. Smith had gone back to school, thus resuming her studies in psychology at some prestigious American university. She had been targeting a bachelor's degree that would take her three academic years to complete after obtaining an associate degree.

As for the exchange program, a couple of things need to be pointed out about it. First, it is worth noting that this program was solely designed for French students, not for foreign students like Onkere. Second, even for French students, there were requirements to be met. However, Pitcherson, an American professor, had come to recognize Onkere's efforts while actively participating in his class. Upon acknowledging the potential of his student from Africa, he explained to him that he could possibly make the magic happen—to send him to America—providing that Onkere met certain requirements unparalleled to those required from French nationals. To that, Onkere asked his professor to spin the bean, so to speak. Here are the requirements: First of all, the protagonist had to be conferred the bachelor's degree. Second, once into the master's program, he had to absolutely do two things. One, he had to validate the master's degree, scoring no less than fifteen out of twenty on the first bloc comprising about six subjects. Two, he had to defend his master's dissertation the same school year, preferably before the deadline of May 15. Relative to the second requirement, he had to score no less than fifteen out of twenty for the defense. Laid out this way, the requirements seemed simple until further explanations were given, as would be done later on.

After their conversation, Onkere worked tirelessly toward getting the first objective accomplished. At the end of that school year, both Onkere and Maldie were successfully conferred bachelor's degrees. This means they automatically moved to the master's degree program. It was also during this year that Onkere learned how to play guitar. The English department had a Music Club supervised by professors from the department.

One day, a friend of Onkere from the Caribbean by the name of Chamsu, a bright, quick thinker from whom Onkere learned a lot, suggested that they attend the club. Once there, one of the professors played a song entitled "You Are My Sunshine," and everyone in the club had to sing it. Those who played an instrument were encouraged to do so. Those who possessed guitars played along. Onkere was so impressed by what he saw in that room, which was that pretty much everyone had and could play guitar except for him. His friend could as well. A week from that day, he bought a guitar with a portion of his stipend money. Ultimately, he started learning to play guitar on his own. What he saw that day encouraged him to learn a new instrument in his life.

Chamsu, a very good friend of Onkere's, was very instrumental in making him fit, so to speak, in academia. He was a well-mannered gentleman who appreciated more British than American culture. He was as intelligent as Onkere. He actually was a black French man originally from Overseas France who, like his friend, was musically inclined with a particular taste for European and British music. Thanks to him, our main protagonist enjoyed some British artists and bands unknown to him at that point, such as Elton John or the Cranberry, just to name a few.

As a student from the English department, Chamsu enjoyed spending his free time at the city hall library, reading books or novels by British authors, given that he majored in British literature and civilization. Together with his friend, they would spend time in bookstores and the university library looking for music CDs and DVDs they could check out for their own enjoyment. One of the things Onkere liked about his friend was the fact that he had lots of novels and that Chamsu would, most of the time, lend them to him, no question asked.

Even if Onkere studied some of those novels in his courses, it definitely was Chamsu who made him appreciate novels such as *Dr. Jekyll and Mr. Hyde* by the Scottish novelist Robert Louis Stevenson or Emily Brontë's *Wuthering Heights*. After reading these novels and many more, both friends also made sure they watched movies resulting from adapting those novels into films.

SUMMERTIME

When summertime finally came, Onkere, who had been in France for two years, told his girlfriend, Ms. Smith, that he would travel back to Mpugu to visit his parents and family members. She made no objection to that idea. In fact, she actually accepted to return there as well. It would be during this summer that the protagonist would introduce his girlfriend to the entire Monray family. Three weeks after being introduced, she returned to the United States, before summer ended, to take care of personal business.

Once back home, everybody Onkere had left was exuberant and delighted to see him back home. However, something strange happened during that trip. Whenever he spoke French, the majority of his friends and family members told him that he sounded like a Frenchman because of his near-French-native accent or diction. I had to explain to those persons, on Onkere's behalf, that he was not doing that on purpose and that he was being influenced by the environment he found himself in.

When he first arrived in France, and more specifically while socializing and interacting within the university settings with his classmates, some of them would sometimes complain about the fact that they could not understand his accent and would, therefore, kindly ask if he could repeat whatever he had just said. Given that Onkere enjoyed speaking in front of the class, he figured that the whole "kindly asking him to repeat himself" phrase was becoming annoying.

In order not to have to repeat himself every time he expressed himself in French, he consciously decided to work toward sounding like a French native every time he spoke. Eventually, before he knew it, it took him less than two years to perfectly sound like a French native.

Before going back to Bonneville for summer, Onkere had already made it possible for his sister Dah to be accepted in a doctoral program at the university he was attending. It needs pointing out that while he was being held back, his little sister kept graduating. Therefore, it should not come as a surprise in Dah's case that she entered the doctoral program before her older brother. Moreover, within the Monray family, school had never been about a competition among family members. It was with great pleasure and joy that he announced to his sister that he had succeeded in enrolling her in the department of philosophy. She had been attending Regina University, living on the same campus her brother was living on, for a whole year before Onkere went on vacation. Dah was very bright with a ladylike personality. She could be very critical of people yet would never put them into boxes. She was a sort of feminist who enjoyed reading and listening to African music. She loved the idea of women's empowerment.

THE UNIQUENESS OF THE MASTER'S DEGREE REQUIREMENTS

Once back to school after his summer vacation, and given the conversation Onkere had the previous year with Professor Pitcherson, he went for a follow-up with the latter. During the course of their discussion, he promised the professor he was going to do what it took to meet the unique requirements he had laid out, hoping to do his part.

He also implied that Professor Pitcherson would honor his words in case he delivered, and Professor Pitcherson agreed.

The challenge then began. Indeed, as mentioned earlier, the challenge was that Onkere had to validate the first bloc, made up of six subjects, scoring no less than fifteen out of twenty. Even so, he had to defend his master's degree dissertation, preferably before May 15, which certainly coincided with the last day all the candidacies should be submitted or examined. That, and he had to score no less than fifteen out of twenty during the defense.

The requirements were challenging. Meeting them unquestionably required discipline, focus, resilience, determination, and, above all, an outstandingly advanced knowledge of the English language.

In reality, the task was almost impossible, and Professor Pitcherson probably knew it. It is as well true that what he asked for made sense, and upon delivery, it would constitute a valuable argument that could not easily be dismissed by his peers. However, technically speaking, the task was enormous for a student to accomplish. Looking back, indeed, Onkere sometimes wonders whether Professor Pitcherson really believed his student could pull it off. As for what had been asked out of him, he was still believing that he might not pull it off. There were obviously many reasons for such a pessimistic viewpoint on his part at that time. The majority of students attending the English master's program back home would not complete it in a two-year period of time. The best students in any master's program, let alone the English one, would complete it in at least three years, whereas the average students would complete it in four or even five years. In France, the best students usually completed it in two years, if not three.

I had never heard of a student, whether in Bonneville or in the university Onkere was attending, who had completed the master's degree program in just one academic year. I am not saying it was not done or might not have been done. Rather, I am saying I had never heard of it. This might mean that completing a master's degree program in such a manner was not a common thing happening all the time. Yet completing it in one academic year was the price Onkere had to pay to be accepted by the committee working with the exchange program meant only for French students. Completing the master's degree in one academic year was, therefore, the ultimate price our protagonist had to pay to be sent to America as an exchange student.

The English master's program was compartmentalized in two blocs. The first one contained about six subjects, while the second bloc dealt with the dissertation part. What is usually done by most students is that during the first year into the program, they make sure to complete its first part. The score required to validate the first bloc is usually ten out of twenty, which is average scoring. The best students start working on the dissertation part during the summer break, so that the next school year, the back and forth of submitting the dissertation drafts to the supervisor begins. In most cases, however, the majority of students generally start writing the dissertation part—meaning the second bloc—the next school year.

One of the reasons the dissertation part takes longer to be completed is because this part has two individuals working together: the student and the supervisor. As such, the student *always* has to be in tune with the supervisor. Also, the back and forth between submitting drafts and getting feedback from the supervisor made it almost impossible for students to complete the master's program even in a two-year period. Additionally, writing any dissertation implies doing research, taking time off, especially knowing that some dissertations might involve fieldwork. Perhaps bearing in mind some of these exogenous factors can help the reader understand the enormous task and challenge facing Onkere. Basically, what exceptional students with amazing skills could accomplish in two years, and average students in three or four years, Onkere had to pull off in just one year—in reality, nine academic months. Even so, despite knowing that the odds could be against him, our main protagonist did not want to let the opportunity slide away. Thinking about the first occasion offered to him by Mr. Jones, his former English instructor during the nineties, he figured out this time that nobody, not even Mister, was going to prevent him from reaching his goal. The reality is that this moment was overdue, and he seized it.

What Onkere accomplished would always remain impressive to me, up to this day. He knew full well that the master degree's year was going to be a determining factor for his future. Given the uniqueness of the requirements already mentioned and the fact that the completion of the second part of the master's degree implied writing a dissertation, he decided to write his on the concept of the American dream. He then discussed the topic right away with Professor Pitcherson, who agreed to supervise the dissertation.

The idea was that Onkere was going to do what it took to write his dissertation while working toward maintaining a solid fifteen out of twenty score on the first bloc.

By making Professor Pitcherson his director, Onkere had unfortunately and indirectly turned down the proposal made to him by Professor Martinez. He was sad about it, while also understanding that life is about making choices that sometimes are not easy to make but that one has the moral obligation to make them. The whole situation affected him a bit because he really and genuinely enjoyed Professor's Martinez courses.

Throughout the year, Onkere collected relevant data and read appropriate books and useful information for his dissertation while regularly attending classes in mornings and afternoons. I would be remiss if I did not mention that the department secretary, Mrs. Joyce, a very nice middle-aged, blond, French lady, was instrumental in helping him fill out all his administrative documents relative to the master's degree program. She would also help him in finding adequate material for his work.

The dissertation was supposed to be written in English, and Onkere loved that idea. In fact, he knew that Professor Pitcherson was American. As a consequence, the feedback was not going to be a problem upon submitting drafts to his appreciation. Midway through the first semester, Onkere had written and submitted almost half of the dissertation to his supervisor. The remaining six months would be devoted to proofreading and editing the text. Onkere would spend entire days between his dormitory room, classes, library, and university restaurant. He devoted the entire year to studying and making sure his academic work met the exceptional requirements imposed upon him. I can remember some of his friends complaining about him being antisocial, spending time in his bedroom studying over weekends, not relaxing at all. Onkere's beard grew unexpectedly longer, and somehow, somewhere, along the way, he neglected his physical appearance. His friend Chamsu was honest enough to tell him he actually did not believe he was going to pull it off. He was not that specific, but everything he did or said proved he did not believe his friend's efforts would be rewarded. Many of his countrymen did not take him seriously. The majority of them did not believe he was going to emerge victorious. Only Dah and Maldie and his girlfriend, Ms. Smith, who was living in America still, were supportive of his efforts. At some point, Onkere became reluctant and did not enjoy hanging out with some of his friends. His sister Dah, Maldie, and Chamsu, his best friends, would complain about some of the behavioral changes they saw happening. The reality is that Onkere did not want to get distracted. He just wanted to do his part by honoring his promise. In the meantime, coincidentally, some of his friends were having issues among them. Onkere was ineluctably put in the middle of that crisis. The protagonist's little sister thought he was not taking care of her or her needs, on the grounds that he was spending much time with some of his friends. In reality, Onkere had been spending more time alone, focusing his energy and attention on working three to four times harder than would excellent master's degree students. The truth is that, at the time these misunderstandings were occurring, Onkere was having doubts about his ability to meet the requirements imposed upon him. To paraphrase Christopher Reeve, in the final analysis, Onkere could be considered a sort of hero—meaning someone who, in spite of weaknesses and doubts, would always go ahead and emerge victorious even though, the majority of the time, he or she would not know the answers or what the outcome might be.

Writing a master's dissertation in academia is indicative that its author has learned advanced grammatical rules, theories, and concepts, learned throughout the years leading to that level. Putting it another way, it sums up all the knowledge one has acquired so far. This is why writing it was at some point frustrating even for Onkere. Let me rewind here again, just to point out that during the entire process of writing his dissertation, Onkere had been discussing with his girlfriend the possibility of her attending his defense in case he prevailed in doing so. She had agreed. What this means is that a week prior to the defense, she arrived in France to support her boyfriend. She, therefore, attended the defense. It was also during that period of time that Dah, Chamsu, and Maldie were officially introduced to the protagonist's girlfriend. A week after the defense, Ms. Smith returned to America, where she was still working toward her own bachelor's degree.

All in all, things progressed smoothly and accordingly. There was such a consistency in his work ethic that things turned out positively. Onkere's dissertation was ready almost a month before May 15. The defense day was scheduled, if I remember correctly, two weeks prior to the deadline. When that day came up, Onkere went to brilliantly make his case in front of two professors and a class half-full of classmates, friends, countrymen, and family members who came to boost and support him. Among them naturally were his sister Dah and his best friends, Maldie and Chamsu.

After more than two hours of presenting his findings and going through the ineluctable series of questions and answers, and cross-examination between him and the professors, Onkere and the audience were nicely and politely asked to exit the classroom. Once out, the audience gossiped about what the sentence could be. Some argued that he did a great job, while others were not so sure about the outcome. Chamsu, Maldie, Dah, and Ms. Smith were positive. Strangely enough, the protagonist himself was less enthusiastic than when he first entered the classroom to make his case. Even though he was interacting with the audience, in reality, his mind and spirit were racing miles away from across the audience, the classroom, and the university where the defense just occurred. He was actually pretending to have a discussion or chat with everyone. The feeling of awkwardness was similar to what he felt back in Bonneville while waiting for the baccalaureate results to come in and publicly be announced.

The audience had been waiting for about thirty minutes when the candidate was summoned to return, facing the jury's deliberation. The verdict was rendered that the candidate had successfully done a good job and was subsequently awarded a solid fifteen out of twenty, a needed score for him to partially meet the requirements imposed upon him. It needs pointing out that the defense of a dissertation can be allowed only if the student has already successfully completed the first bloc part of the master's program. Putting it another way, it was because Onkere had already successfully validated the first bloc composed of six different subjects that the department authorized the defense to proceed. There as well, as it turned out, Onkere did the magic by maintaining a solid fifteen-out-of-twenty grade point average at the end of the academic year. All in all, the main protagonist remarkably pulled it off by meeting the requirements. These results were naturally submitted to Professor Pitcherson, his supervisor, in charge of the exchange program dealing with American universities.

At the end of May, Professor Pitcherson delivered the good news to Onkere, informing him that, having seen all the efforts and sacrifices he went through and the excellent results of his performances, it had been decided that he would be part of the exchange program. This meant that he would be benefiting from the exchange program regardless of him not being a French national. He would thus be attending an American university as a teaching assistant. Upon hearing the news, Onkere contained himself. He thanked his professor and went to the dormitory to inform his sister as well as his best two friends. Everyone was euphoric. The news did not sink in right away. Onkere was still not fully grasping what was happening to him. He was emotionally confused. The young man from Akaga City was still morally, spiritually, and physically worn out.

Professor Pitcherson had delivered what he too promised, and it would be an understatement to say that the protagonist was not delighted regardless of the mixed feelings he was experiencing at that point. Less than a week from exchanging views with Professor Pitcherson, the travel documents were issued. Everything was almost perfect. All the needed documentation was there. However, before traveling to America, Onkere made sure that his parents, more specifically Mister, his father, were informed. He then traveled back to Toshville to personally inform his parents about the news. Once back home, he did just that. This time around, he received no objection from either of his parents. In fact, they were more than delighted for him, considering that more than a decade ago, Mister had rejected the proposal made by Mr. Jones, Onkere's former English instructor, to take him to America. After accepting the good news, once again, Mister reminded his son of his obligation and responsibility to return home upon completion of his teaching in America. Mister furthermore insisted on that requirement of his, especially considering that Onkere's brother Randy had already returned home upon brilliantly defending his doctoral dissertation. Dr. Randy was now a law professor at Bonneville University.

The exchange program Onkere was participating in was between Regina University and Charles-Raymond University. As an exchange student from a French university, Onkere, who had just been conferred a master of arts degree in English, would be teaching French at an American university. Prior to traveling, he was told that the exchange program would last for a year. He was told that there was a possibility for students to prolong their stay if they so chose. Then, once again, there would be requirements to be met.

One of the requirements would be based on how well the new teaching assistant carried his or her class. It would also be dependent on how well the student-lecturer relationship went and how well he or she performed throughout the academic year. Onkere had no problem performing. Thus, he was delighted to travel to America.

CHAPTER 7

Teaching Abroad: America

I say to you today, my friends, so even though we face the
difficulties of today and tomorrow, I still have a dream.
It is a dream deeply rooted in the American dream. I
have a dream that one day this nation will rise up and
live out the true meaning of its creed: "We hold these
truths to be self-evident: that all men are created equal."
—Martin Luther King Jr.

BOSTON

Onkere was so highly spirited and motivated when he got
to Boston. He had a sense that his life was meaningful
and that he actually was accomplishing something. He just
graduated and, upon receiving his master's degree in Europe,
was traveling to America to share not only his knowledge
and know-how but also the French and Francophone
cultures. The sole idea of sharing knowledge was amazingly
impressive to him.

As for the trip, he had to be in Boston no later than August 15, one of the documents stated. Bearing this requirement in mind, he arrived at Boston airport on August 5, giving himself exactly ten days to get organized and have the ball rolling.

Prior to his arrival, however, Mrs. Joyce, the department secretary from Regina University, had gotten in touch with her counterpart from the French department of Charles-Raymond University, one of the most prestigious universities in America, where Onkere was supposed to be teaching French.

She had provided him with all the necessary information relative to accommodation. Basically, he had the address and street he would be staying on. All he did then was get a cab to take him to the location. As it turned out, he was going to stay on Lynn Street. Once there, he knew where to find the key to unlock the door, which he did. He then surreptitiously got in and went to a bedroom already made available and waiting for him. Onkere made it to America, realizing a dream deferred, to paraphrase Langston Hughes. This dream had been instilled and embedded in his brain since his first English instructor openly discussed with him the possibility of traveling to America. A deferred dream that inspired him as well to write a master's degree dissertation on the topic of the American dream. A deferred dream that, almost fifteen years after the day it came to be, would finally be realized by none other than Onkere himself. What a story. What a dedication to a dream. Was it a dream to begin with?

The next day, upon his arrival, Onkere did what he always did whenever he got to a new place, which is that he went out to visit the town. This time, he walked southward across Lynn Street, his main location. After about one and a half hours, he walked back to his place. The next day, he crossed Lynn Street. He moved two or three blocks away from that location and walked farther away, as far as he could, toward downtown, where he saw for the first time the impressive tall old building. Across the street from that building, he saw another tall building, home to the French department where he would be teaching French for five consecutive academic years.

The city, as well as the places he was observing that day, appeared to be beautifully nice. The city seemed quiet, whereas the majority of the buildings were a bit high compared to what he had been accustomed to.

CHARLES-RAYMOND UNIVERSITY: YEAR 1

On August 15, which was a Monday, he went to the university and was welcomed by a very nice white lady in her midsixties by the name of Maryrosa. She provided him with everything he needed to have and know about the institution at that time. She also explained to him the way the French department was functioning. Of course, Onkere thanked Maryrosa and went back to his place. The fall semester had not started yet.

The next morning, he went back to the university for a sort of training. As a matter of fact, all the exchange students coming to Charles-Raymond University as teaching assistants, or TAs, had to take pedagogy classes and undergo training, during which they were basically educated on how to teach foreign languages in American settings. The training lasted for two weeks before class started. It was a very important seminar and training. It allowed teaching assistants, especially new ones, to quickly understand the American educational system at the university level. It furthermore helped them realize what was expected of them, what their duties and obligations were, how to interact with students, and the dynamic that had to prevail at all times between TAs and students. The seminars were also a way to check and measure TAs' level of understanding of the English language.

In fact, no foreign-language instructor can teach at any American university without mastering the English language. If they do, they are likely to get into trouble, because the majority of students, as will be explained later on, take foreign languages not necessarily because they like them but because they are required to do so. During those seminars, TAs were warned about sexual harassment and how they could constitute a serious crime, ultimately bringing their contracts to an end, on top of the litigation that could potentially result from lawsuits likely to be filed by any of the victims. Given that teaching assistants were not experienced instructors, they were told each of them would be teaching under the supervision of a faculty professor, whom they would report to for suggestions, advice, or any complaint. As for Mrs. Maryrosa, she right away told Onkere which professor did what, where and when, as well as the ones he should be aware of.

A week before the fall semester started, we had already been given our schedules, and I am sure that Onkere received his as well. In fact, his schedule indicated that he would be teaching three classes per day. He had been assigned to teach French I for beginners in two classes and Intermediate French II in one class. Needless to say, he was more than ready to hit the ground running and take on that monumental responsibility. The first day of class, he felt great and energized. He had prepared his course and was ready to go share it with students. On that first day, he knew he had to introduce himself and pretty much get to know the students. After introducing himself, he told the students what the class was going to be about and what he expected of them. He also reassured them that they would have a great time together. The introduction was carried out with near-native French accent. Given that the majority of students were not familiar with the French language, Onkere had to, from time to time, switch to English so as to explain and expand on what he had just said, after receiving polite requests from several students.

After he introduced himself, the floor was given to the students so they could introduce themselves and tell why they had picked French, this foreign language. As could be expected, reasons were different from one student to the other. Out of the thirty students attending that class, about five or seven had picked French because they actually liked foreign languages, particularly French and its culture. They really wanted to be knowledgeable in the French language. The rest of the students picked French because it was a requirement for them. This meant that they basically did not like the language. Rather, they had to pick a foreign language in order to graduate, as part of their curriculum. And they randomly picked it. The reasons why students pick subjects is crucial because, as an instructor, Onkere understood whether the students would have a motive or reason to be motivated and engaged during class activities. In fact, from students' introductions, I knew right away that Onkere would have a class where no student would seriously be working on French with the intent of acquiring the tools and grammatical elements that would allow them to, later on, master the French language. That being said, some students were surprisingly happy to have a young, energized, handsome man as their French instructor, freshly coming from France, and not an old French lady, as many had expected. That same day, Onkere had to do the same exercise in two additional classes—first in his second Intermediate French I and later on in his Intermediate French II. There again, after he introduced himself, the floor was given to the students. Basically, the answers given to justify the reasons why French had been chosen were pretty much the same, even though those given by students attending Intermediate French II were nuanced. In fact, some of them either had been to Paris or had enjoyed French music and movies. As such, either way, they felt some sort of connection with the French language and needed to deepen their knowledge of the language. Even for those who picked it as part of the requirement, still, they expressed a willingness to be open to the possibility of considering learning the language as they would for any other subject. This was encouraging for the instructor.

At the end of that first tiring day of class, Onkere anticipated that he might run into misunderstandings with students from his morning French class. Many factors were established to make that likely to happen. That first French class of his was supposed to start every morning at eight o'clock. What this meant was that by six thirty, four days out of five, he had to get up and be ready, given that he had to walk to the university even though his place was not that far away from the building where the French department was located. The office that he shared with an American instructor was located on the building's third level. The second factor, in retrospect, was the fact that the majority of the students attending his French class had just graduated from high school. They were probably taught French by licensed instructors rather than native French or near-native speakers like Onkere, who had lived and studied in France and had just come from there. The final factor, and not the least of them, was the fact that the majority of the students were young, spoiled kids from different racial backgrounds.

Less than three months into Onkere teaching his courses, students from his morning French class started complaining about the fact that the protagonist was not being understanding because he had been giving them what some considered to be failing grades, which in all actuality were B and C grades. One day, while he was giving students their tests back, one of them stood up. She confronted him about the fact that he was not taking into consideration all the efforts they were putting into studying French, this foreign language to them. Moreover, she argued that it was easy for him to be strict and tough on them because he was the instructor and had lived and studied in France. She basically suggested that Onkere should relax and take things easy. She passionately expressed herself in English. Following his student's complaint, which was shared by the majority of the students, Onkere, who had never been confronted by a student, thought she had crossed a line confronting him the way she did, especially her using what he perceived as a condescending tone. On that note, he basically addressed the issue right away. Instead of replying specifically to that student, he honestly told the entire class that he would never give them undeserved grades. He also suggested that if they wanted A and A+ grades, they should work a little bit harder. On top of that, the instructor told his students that he was there not to please them but to teach them a foreign language.

For having honestly given them feedback, Onkere had sinned. As a sinner, metaphorically speaking, he had to pay for the crime he had committed. In fact, the next morning, the atmosphere was rotten, and not many students were willing to participate during class activities. Five students or fewer than that figure participated. Everyone could see that something had gone wrong the previous day. The following morning, Onkere's course supervisor summoned him into her office. She basically told him to cool off and blamed him for what had transpired in his morning class. According to her, the instructor had been unprofessionally engaging in unnecessary discussions with students. She argued that, as an instructor, Onkere should not have openly expressed himself the way he did, basically telling the students the truth by way of asking them to work a bit harder so as to get deserved grades. For someone whose entire life had revolved around hardships he ultimately overcame, no matter the time it took him to prevail, his supervisor's arguments came as a shock to him. Right there, he understood what the expression *culture shock* meant. She then asked him to find a way to satisfy his students, going forward, if he really wanted the misunderstanding resolved. In order for Onkere's supervisor to make sure he had what it took to teach French, an unexpected camera crew was sent into his morning class to videotape him while teaching a course. Along with the crew members came the head of the department, who was there to monitor the videotaping. A day later, after videotaping the instructor, a three-page written assessment of his teaching and interaction with the students was handed to him by the department secretary. That report, written in the English language by the head of the department himself, described how Onkere brilliantly conducted his course, highlighting the different grammatical aspects and points that were successfully taught on that day. It also stated how orally and fluently he could express himself, with such an easiness that made the interaction between him and his students go smoothly. In fact, it is my belief that two things were being looked at during the videotaping. One, to see how well he could speak and teach French. Two, how well he could interact with students and how they would respond to his teachings. At the end of the day, the instructor performed excellently well. The report concluded that he basically did an excellent job, that no deficiency whatsoever was found that could lead to questioning his intellectual abilities in speaking French, and that he had what it took to keep teaching that foreign language. In all honesty, had Onkere's performance been poor, there is no doubt in my mind that his contract would have been terminated right away.

That same day, once back at his place, the French instructor reflected upon what had just transpired. He, later on, would express how he felt to a friend and colleague by the name of Tall, whom he had met during the training sessions they underwent prior to the starting of the fall semester. Onkere had become close to him since the starting of the school year. Tall had been living in Boston for about two or three years by the time Onkere met him. He had also been teaching French for about the same amount of time while working toward his PhD. So, he obviously knew a lot in terms of how specifically the department worked. Therefore, Onkere most of the time relied on him for advice. Additionally, he had been living in America longer than Onkere. Tall was very bright, caring, and understanding, and, above all, he remained calm under pressure.

As for the whole videotaping situation, Onkere explained to his colleague that it was kind of surreal. In fact, he argued, never in a million years did he think that he would, one day, be videotaped because his knowledge of the French language was being questioned on the grounds that he had told students the truth about what they needed to do in order to get deserved grades.

The cultural shock Onkere referred to was due to the fact that at Charles-Raymond University, he had been condescendingly confronted by a student whom he thought was not in a position to confront him. And, by position, I mean academically speaking. In fact, confronting Onkere, as that student of his did, would never have happened if they were in a different university setting. The in-your-face type of attitude exhibited by that student of his was remarkably troublesome to the young French instructor. Moreover, that type of attitude would never have been allowed anyplace else. Onkere took this cultural shock the hardest way. Never in a million years did he think that students could literally demand specific grades from any instructor. The following days and weeks, Onkere softened his approach and succeeded in bringing tranquility into the class, as was suggested by his course supervisor. All in all, things were normal again. He did not have any trouble with the other two classes. Rather, two or three students from his morning class, together with students from his other two classes, expressed regrets and apologized to him. Some of them even felt an injustice had been done to him.

Among those students was a young nice man whose friendship I enjoyed. He originally was from another state and had come to pursue his studies in Boston, on the grounds that it was a calmer city in contrast to the state he came from, where a day would not go by without some young men getting gunned down. In a word, he had run away from insecurity and police brutality, features associated with the state he was from. Also, it needs mentioning that he was more open-minded than the majority of the students. He seemed more mature. He had traveled the world more than the majority of his classmates. Additionally, he was biracial, in terms of his mother being an American and his father of Chinese origin. So, his cultural heritage made him more sympathetic toward his instructor even though he was born and raised in America. As far as the whole incident, in retrospect, if I were Onkere, maybe I should not have engaged in the kind of honest narrative he shared with his students. The whole incident remains indicative of cultural differences about how things are carried out within two different educational systems. That would be my takeaway, which I have no doubt Onkere would share. That incident also constituted a ground, allowing the protagonist to tour America in order to try to have a broader understanding of the country's diverse cultures. In that regard, he initiated a series of trips during the following spring break.

He traveled more than three times in less than two months to Chicago, where his cousin Chris, the man who took him and his brother Randy back to their roots, was now living with his fiancée, who years later would become his wife. During one of those trips to Chicago, he learned about the important role played by Jesse Jackson, who, during the civil rights movement, was one of the closest advisers to Dr. Martin Luther King Jr. Apart from his cousin, Onkere also had two friends from Chicago whom he visited at some point.

As the school year was nearing its end, during that same spring break, Onkere traveled to Atlanta, Georgia, to visit Dr. Martin Luther King Jr. Center for Nonviolence. On the day of his arrival, he also visited Dr. Martin Luther King Jr.'s grave, as well as the iconic Ebenezer Baptist Church where both father and son preached. The three-day trip constituted an opportunity for the French instructor to visit the house Dr. King actually grew up in. It serves as a sort of museum now. The trip was like a pilgrimage the young man from Akaga City felt he had to make. In fact, back in Toshville in Africa, he had not only grown up publicly performing well-known speeches and sermons by Dr. Martin Luther King Jr., but he had also studied and read a lot of books and watched documentaries about the civil rights movement and some well-known personalities associated with this movement. So, in a sense, it was fitting that once in America, the French instructor went on that pilgrimage. He talked with some of the people who were part of this movement. He even made a home video of his trip to Atlanta, discussing the civil rights movement, Dr. Martin Luther King Jr., and what the trip meant to him.

Initially, the protagonist came to America for a one-year teaching position as a teaching assistant. The trip overseas, for the international exchange student he was, coming from France, also meant an opportunity for him to do research and collect data and any information he could possibly gather that would ultimately help him while working toward the doctoral dissertation. Putting it another way, the French instructor, who was likely going to return to France, was hoping to write his doctoral dissertation on the civil rights movement. Therefore, being in America meant that not only would he be teaching French to students, but he had also to make his own research, because, after all, he was first and foremost a graduate student. That same year, he went to visit museums in Kansas City. This time, he traveled with his colleague Tall. Once there, he did some additional research related to the history of African Americans and Native Americans.

As the year was drawing to its end, the French instructor was told that there would be a possibility for him to stay, if the reports from both his students and course supervisor were positive. For that to happen, the reports had to distinctly establish that he met the requirements needed to maintain, prolong, and renew the contract as well as the teaching position. In order to maintain a teaching position at Charles-Raymond University, and I can only assume nationwide, teaching assistants have to be evaluated by students on their ability to teach, communicate, and conduct classes and whether the students would recommend the teaching assistant's course to other students.

These criteria and many more were some of the elements that the students had to evaluate instructors on.

The instructors whose percentage scores were not above the required figure had their contracts terminated. Once the results are in, the course supervisor reviews them to determine the teaching assistant's fate, so to speak. It turned out that Onkere did an excellent job. Strangely enough, even a large number of students from his eight o'clock class had a positive opinion of him. On the question relative to whether his class should be recommended to other students, those who answered yes explained that the students taking his class needed to make sure they liked the French language. They suggested that students should not take it just because it is a requirement for them, given that the French instructor was serious about teaching his course. Onkere had very positive evaluations from his two other classes as well. All in all, his contract was extended for another year. He had the choice of staying in America or returning to Europe. He had to make his decision known at due time. Before the end of May, he had already, like the majority of his colleagues, made his decision known. He was going to extend his stay. In the process, he asked to get enrolled in the department as a graduate student. In fact, he had come to America not as an international student but rather as a scholar. Therefore, he was actually asking for a status change. Upon his request, the department authorities accepted his proposal, and he had to go through certain exams in order to access the graduate program, which he did. In order to be accepted into the graduate college, regardless of Onkere being a graduate international student and teaching assistant, he had to take and pass some tests. He was required to take the Test of English as a Foreign Language (TOEFL) and the Graduate Record Examinations (or GRE).

The first test is a kind of standardized examination that is taken mainly by international students whose native language is not English. Regardless of Onkere holding a master's degree in English, he was obligated to take the graduate college requirement. Naturally, he scored high in the three different compartments of the examination: writing, listening, and speaking, if I am not mistaken. I am not sure what the third component was though. As for the Graduate Record Examinations, or GRE, he passed it with flying colors. The GRE was a bit longer than the TOEFL in the sense that it actually covered a range of humanities as well as scientific topics, such as general culture, philosophy, mathematics, biology, chemistry, and the like. The examination consisted of several multiple-choice questions and writing essays in all of those areas. Here again, I am not sure about what the components of each section were. All in all, things went well, and he was accepted in the master's degree program.

FAMILY MEMBERS

In the meantime, Dah, his little sister, was now a third-year doctoral student. As such, she was almost more than halfway through working on her dissertation. His other little sister Opy had just started her doctoral program. Back home, his immediate little sister, Yogi, had just finished her bachelor's degree in sciences and was looking for employment openings and opportunities. Dr. Randy was still teaching at Bonneville University School of Law. He had also entered politics by now. His little brother Tom had been working closely with their brother Randy. Back to Toshville, his sister Eyila was now a proud, self-employed businesswoman, managing a chain of restaurants and pubs, while his eldest sister, Djoka, had graduated from nursing school and was working for one of the most important hospitals of the region in terms of technology. She was an accomplished and successful real estate businesswoman. The twin sisters were still doing their own things. Mariella had enrolled in the military forces, while Olivia, who by now had given birth to a beautiful daughter, had unexpectedly become a national musical sensation touring the country. Meanwhile, his youngest sister, Claudia, was about to graduate from high school, upon which she would travel to France to pursue her studies. She was very clever, smart, and wise. She was an effective communicator and listener who, like the majority of her siblings, was a feminist who entertained the idea of being judged on her merit as well as the content of her bubbly personality. She was caring and looked out for the poor among us. Basically, everyone in Onkere's family was active, doing something. Bearing this reality in mind, our protagonist understood that he had to be fast and get done with school. In fact, words were circulating a lot that his father was getting tired of him being abroad for such a long time. The reality was that his father, Mister, was getting older and older. And the more he was getting older, the sicker he became.

By the time these events occurred, the French instructor had been dating his girlfriend, Ms. Smith, for about quite some time. Together, they had spent time in Europe, America, and Africa. Upon his arrival in America, the two of them had reconnected. In fact, Ms. Smith had been living, coincidentally, not that far from Boston. She actually went to welcome her boyfriend at the airport on the day of his initial arrival. She and her parents were going to be very instrumental in the French instructor's adventure in America.

Now, I need to rewind here by saying that when Ms. Smith left her boyfriend in France, upon visiting him during his defense, she got pregnant. She would give birth to their first daughter during the following summer, less than a year after Onkere's arrival in America. Their firstborn would be named Stinky Peedles—the apple of the couple's eyes. She would turn out to be very smart and very bright. Stinky Peedles loved music and practiced a multitude of sports. She also practiced dance and gymnastics. She speaks more than two international languages, just like her parents. She is a soft-spoken adolescent young lady now, with a strong-willed spirit, who knows what she wants in life. She is the protector of her siblings and serves as a guide in times of need. She loves both of her parents dearly as well as both of her grandpas and grandmas.

CHARLES-RAYMOND UNIVERSITY: YEAR 2

While teaching the following fall semester, the French instructor, who had excellently learned to play guitar, was invited to do just that: play guitar in his colleagues' classes. He was gladly accompanied by one of his students who also knew how to play the instrument. That student of his was experienced and played guitar well, to the satisfaction of the instructor. He was almost a musician. A nice young man, that student, and his French instructor would essentially play a French repertoire by singers such as Joe Dassin,

Francis Cabrel, and Johnny Halliday, to name just a few. One of the main objectives was to learn and teach French through music and enjoyment, a learning methodology the French instructor learned years ago while leading English Clubs back home.

The songs that were played, most of the time, were Joe Dassin's "Salut les Amoureux," Francis Cabrel's "L'Encre de Tes Yeux," Halliday's "Le Penitencier" and "Marie." We would sometimes play songs like "You Are My Sunshine," which the French instructor adored playing. One day, while they were rehearsing, the French instructor learned from his student that Johnny Halliday's "Le Penitencier" was actually a remix, so to speak, of The Animals' "House of the Rising Sun." It was an amazing teaching moment for Onkere.

The same academic year, he still lived on Lynn Street and was now more or less accustomed to the way things were being carried out and managed within the department at the university. On top of being a teaching assistant, he was also now an international student attending the same department and having some of his colleagues as his professors. Regardless of his new status, he was assigned three classes. Like all the teaching assistants, he would have one additional day during which he would conduct oral examinations for students from other teaching assistants' classes. The oral examination was part of the French curriculum. Its objective was to allow instructors to measure students' fluency in French. Before the fall semester started, once again, Onkere, Tall, the rest of the teaching assistants, and I attended teaching seminar sessions, during which we were politely reminded of what it meant to teach foreign languages in an American setting as well as the strategies that should be used to wisely engage students while encouraging them to like the language being taught and participate in our respective classes. I must confess that those seminars were of incredible help to Onkere as far as his teaching was concerned. As for me, I just loved attending those seminars.

THE MASTER'S DEGREE: YEAR 1

As international students attending the master's degree program, we were requested, as graduate students, by the graduate college to take at least two courses from other departments. Naturally, having a background in English, Onkere took two graduate classes from the English department, picking two courses entitled Advanced Readings in Black Culture and African American Autobiography. The two courses he enjoyed the most from his program were Teaching and Learning Foreign Language and Comparative Stylistics. While the first focused on pedagogy and strategies to teach foreign languages within different settings and environments, the latter dealt with translation techniques between the French and English languages. That particular course was taught to students from the English departments in France and Mpugu as well.

The courses Advanced Readings in Black Culture and African American Autobiography were taught by an African American professor for whom Onkere had tremendous respect. He was the only African American who taught the protagonist English during the entire course of his academic years. That is part of what made Onkere have a special bond with him. During the two years he attended the professor's classes, the two bonded and ended up becoming good friends. Onkere would, on many occasions, seek advice from him on many topics and situations school related. More importantly, however, the said professor had a cutting-edge understanding of the history of African Americans as it related to the whole American culture. He had intensively written on many subjects ranging from jazz music to questions of black identity in America, race relations, and many more. He was an open-minded professor who was naturally interested in Onkere's story, background, and country of origin. A very nice gentleman, the said professor was demanding when it came to school work. He insisted that his instructions be followed while working on our assignments. While the course Teaching and Learning Foreign Language was taught by professors from the education department, Comparative Stylistics was taught to us by a French professor. He was an introverted person, very gentle, very quiet yet strict when it came to school work. Being a French native, the said professor understood better African students attending his classes and seminars, given the historical relationship between African French-speaking countries and France.

The majority of the American professors teaching at the department were knowledgeable. They spoke French fluently with a certain distinctive American accent. They were more than open-minded, flexible, and fair to all the students regardless of their sex, gender, sexual orientation, race, or place of origin. There was a sense of tolerance, acceptance, belonging, and togetherness, with everyone acknowledging and knowing, in the process, what their place really was.

Onkere had a very productive year both as teaching assistant and international student. He was successful in his own class and moved up to the second level of the master's degree program. As a teaching assistant, the majority of the students' evaluations from all his three classes were positive. This meant that his teaching contract was renewed for another school year, and the third one. In order to make both ends meet, he and his friend Tall decided to teach summer classes. In order to kill time during weekends, Onkere, who had perfected his guitar playing style, would play the instrument while singing songs such as "You Are My Sunshine," which he first heard while living in Europe. He would also play John Denver's "Country Roads" and Bob Dylan's "Blowin' in the Wind," songs he first heard while socializing with the Joneses around the late eighties, back in Toshville Mpugu.

While all of this was happening, two years before, signs of trouble had been noticed in the US economy. By this time, campaign rallies and meetings for the American presidential election, which was still two years away, were already in full swing. From both political parties, candidates had already announced the run for the presidency. They were already known to the American public. From the Republican side, former Massachusetts Governor Mitt Romney, Mike Huckabee of Arkansas, and Senator John McCain of Arizona were among the leading candidates. In the meantime, former North Carolina senator John Edwards, former senator Barack Obama of Illinois, and former New York senator Hillary Clinton were among the candidates getting respect and admiration from the Democratic side. Therefore, their candidacies needed to be taken seriously.

CHARLES-RAYMOND UNIVERSITY: YEAR 3

When the next school year started, as usual, teaching assistants went through the training sessions followed by class and schedule partition. This time, I believe, Onkere, a well-trained and experienced teaching assistant, was assigned four classes. One of them was an advanced one. He had a new textbook for the advanced class and hoped to do a good job with it. In the meantime, as an international student, he needed to get ready, making sure he was going to graduate. As I pointed out earlier, a master's degree program entails two parts or blocs. Here again, the first part was made up of about eight subjects, whereas the second part dealt with writing a dissertation. It was called "complementary work." Here as well, the complementary work could only be dealt with following the successful completion of the first part. Onkere knew it because he had already gone through this process before.

As the school year was getting near its end, the political campaign was in full speed. Given that that year was going to be an election year and that Boston was going to be among the first ones to hold primaries nationwide, administrative authorities anticipated the likelihood of the school year being disrupted at some point by politicians who would come on campus trying to communicate their agenda to the youth.

THE MASTER'S DEGREE: YEAR 2

It was in a presidential election context that the school year was carried out. As an international student, Onkere did the best he could to successfully complete the written and first part of his master's program. He also did the best he possibly could to get done with the complementary work on time. By the time he was ready to undergo the oral examination, school was out. The oral examination was then scheduled for the fall semester of the following year. Meanwhile, during that school year, America finally witnessed the worst economic crisis the nation had ever experienced since the Great Depression of 1929. The crisis impacted almost all major sectors of activities. Firms and factories were shutting down, sending jobs overseas. The unemployment rate increased, and universities were downsizing or simply laying off. In the department, some teaching assistants were told that, due to the dire economic situation the nation was witnessing, some of us would not see our contracts renewed for another term. We were also told that we would be notified separately at due time. And they did. Onkere was one of those teaching assistants whose contract was not renewed. Given that he had been scheduled to make his master's defense some date around the end of fall semester the following year, his contract, however, was extended.

CHARLES-RAYMOND UNIVERSITY: YEAR 4

In the meantime, things between him and his girlfriend were going well. They had been talking about moving in together, so much so that after graduating, they definitely moved in together. By the time these events occurred, Stinky Peedles, the apple of their eyes, their beautiful daughter, and the firstborn out of their children, was about to turn five years old. Onkere, his amazingly beautiful girlfriend, and their daughter were all three now living in North Liberty, located about thirty minutes from Boston.

While the French instructor was still teaching at Charles-Raymond University, the then junior senator from the great state of Illinois came on campus more than three times. One of these times, while he was teaching one of his classes, his students told him that the junior senator would be on campus and that all the students felt like attending his political meeting. Given that his students were enthusiastically motivated, the French instructor allowed them to go hear what the senator had to say. The instructor himself seized that opportunity to attend the political meeting as well. Another time, the senator came to town to campaign. That time around, the political rally was held at some hotel forty-five minutes away from the university. The French instructor and his colleague Tall suggested that they both attend the meeting, which they did.

During that meeting, both Onkere and his colleague had a chance to exchange a few words while shaking hands with the junior senator from Illinois. They basically praised him and expressed how optimistic they were about his campaign and wished him good luck. A mutual friend to both Tall and Onkere had told them the previous day that the senior senator from Texas was going to make an appearance in Boston the next day during a book-signing tour at a bookstore downtown, not far from the university. On that day, Onkere and his friend walked across the street from the university to the bookstore, where the latter ended up purchasing the senator's book just to get a chance to chitchat with him. While his friend was exchanging words with the senator, Onkere, who was standing there next to his friend, took that opportunity to wish the senator good luck on his campaign. The senator picked up on his slight French accent and asked him where he was from and what he was doing in town. Naturally, Onkere told the senator that he was an international student working toward a master's degree while teaching at the university. He went on, telling the senator that he was from Mpugu, an African country located on the continent's western part. To that, the senator, in an honest manner that characterizes him, apologized for not knowing where Mpugu was located on the African continent. It was a very nice and touching moment. For a while, the senior senator from Texas had forgotten about American politics but genuinely branched out, discussing international affairs, so to speak, with an African international teaching assistant.

CHARLES-RAYMOND UNIVERSITY: YEAR 5

Tall and Onkere closely followed that presidential election. Had it not been for the fact that the protagonist, who is an American politics enthusiast, was teaching while working on his master's dissertation, he could have easily been part of the junior senator's, from the great state of Illinois, presidential campaign organizers. The senator's message of change and well-formulated strategies and cutting-edge knowledge of the issues made his campaign so attractive to young people, to such a degree that even some international graduate students from the university Onkere was attending became part of the senator's campaign organizers for that state. Apart from Tall and his own girlfriend he would discuss politics with, the French instructor would also eagerly discuss candidates' strategies, strengths, and weaknesses with his future father-in-law, whom he respectfully refers to by a special nickname, despite being discouraged to do so by his girlfriend's mother.

A multitasking theologian, my future father-in-law, Dr. Chuck, happens to be one of the most open-minded conservatives I have ever known. Politically speaking, he sides with Republican candidates. He also enjoys speculating about American and international politics with the French instructor. He is kind, gentle, and very bright. He enjoys listening to music from the fifties and the sixties. He also enjoys the sound of birds while reading a good book. Among the American famous people who showed up on the campus on behalf of the junior senator from the great state of Illinois, while the presidential campaign was in full mode, was one of the most well-known and respected black intellectuals in America, by the name of Kole. And also Bete, one of the best and acclaimed Hollywoodian actors. They both came on campus at different times. First came Professor Kole. He made the trip to Boston to mobilize the small black and Latino communities living on campus.

The day he came, I informed both Onkere and his friend Tall that he would be on campus. I even suggested that they needed to go check him out, which they did. Professor Kole eloquently spoke about the reasons why he strongly believed in the senator's message of change and hope. He furthermore addressed reasons why he thought the junior senator from Illinois was the best candidate. In fact, he argued that his economic policies were likely to improve the living conditions of not only African Americans but also

Latinos as well as poor white Americans. He furthermore talked about the senator's family and the kind of values he believed the senator had in common with the majority of Americans from various socioeconomic backgrounds.

The same card was also played by actor Bete, who addressed some of the reasons why African American actors like himself appreciated seeing the senator running for the presidency. More importantly, he eloquently spoke about the senator's youth and emphasized reasons why the young generation needed to support and vote for his candidate. Once again, his message of change and hope was indicative of him being the change and hope Americans from all backgrounds, races, and political parties had been waiting for after the previous failed presidency. The rally was held in open air. Lots of white, black, and Latino students, including Onkere, attended it. Meanwhile, Ms. Smith, by now Onkere's fiancée, and their daughter, Stinky Peedles, got a chance to attend one of the many rallies held by the senator from New York City. At the end of that meeting, they both had a chance to shake hands with the senator. While all of these presidential campaign meetings and rallies were being held nationally and domestically, on the university campus, the French instructor kept on working toward his doctoral dissertation.

CHAPTER 8

The Doctorate

A journey to a thousand miles begins with a single step.
—Lao Tzu

THE DOCTORAL PROGRAM

Onkere got in touch with two professors from France to see whether they would be willing to supervise his doctoral dissertation in the field of American studies. At this point, I feel morally compelled to explain that Onkere's two-year master's degree program was financed by the income he was earning from teaching at the university while attending his own classes at the same time. Therefore, once the teaching assistant contract was terminated upon honorably obtaining his second master's degree, while maintaining over a 3.70-grade point average, he no longer had any source of income. Consequently, the former French instructor could no longer afford to pay for a PhD program in America. It could be argued that he could have. Yet, for that to have happened, he would have had to find a job first. Unfortunately, following the US economic crisis of that year, no one was hiring. Plus, all he wanted to do and knew to do, at that time, was teaching, while major American universities were downsizing. So, it was fitting that he returned to France to pursue his doctoral studies.

No laying off or downsizing of any sort was going to derail this resilient and determined African young man from his objective, especially when he was almost there. His goal at this stage was to get a PhD in the field of American studies. The department secretary was genuinely sad to see Onkere leaving. But there was nothing she could have done. The French instructor comforted her and told her it was all right that he had to leave. By this time, Onkere, Stinky Peedles, and his fiancée, Ms. Smith, had moved to another residency.

Before heading back to France, Onkere, as already mentioned, got in touch with two professors from two different institutions. The first was from the Sorbonne University, and the second from Pierrette University. The professor from the latter institution agreed to supervise the dissertation and asked for a meeting with him. He would later on travel to Pierretteville, a typical French college town, not only to get register but also to fill out the administrative documents. The Sorbonne University professor, to speak of him, agreed to supervise Onkere's dissertation only if the latter started over by enrolling in the English master's program, which Onkere emphatically rejected.

Once in Pierretteville, he met with Professor LeGrand, a blond, medium-sized, white French man, very reserved and quite knowledgeable in English and American studies. Both men talked for about two hours, during which questions were asked about why Onkere had decided to get his doctorate degree at Pierrette University, one of the most prestigious French universities, and not in an American one, considering he had been living in America for quite some time. Onkere explained to the professor the reasons already mentioned, relative to the downsizing of different sectors of activities in the US following the economic crisis. Professor LeGrand then proceeded to confirm that he would be supervising his doctoral dissertation, and both men talked for additional minutes.

During the course of their discussion, the professor explained to him that day that in order to be considered serious work, given the area being covered within the American civilization, the type of dissertation underway required fieldwork. Therefore, the doctoral student and former French instructor was nicely encouraged to venture out of France to conduct interviews with some actors implicated in the civil rights movement, as well as those who had a cutting-edge knowledge of American politics, political parties, and ideologies, main areas to be covered by the dissertation.

To these suggestions, Onkere offered no objection whatsoever, knowing that the fieldwork could be done only in America. He felt in tune with these suggestions precisely because he had made it clear to the professor that he would not be living in Pierretteville. Rather, he would be residing in America while working toward his dissertation, because he was in a serious relationship and had left his fiancée and daughter back there. The professor had accepted that explanation as well as its implication. At the end of that first encounter, all was said and agreed upon. One of the aspects made clear was the fact that Professor LeGrand asked for drafts to be mailed to him so he could go through them. Following the corrections, the doctoral student must be in Pierretteville to discuss the way forward till completion of the writing part.

The doctoral student understood that even though he would remain in America, he nevertheless had to be in Pierretteville at least two times during a school year till completion of the doctoral dissertation. English and American civilization was the field the former French instructor from Charles-Raymond University was pursuing his PhD in. As a consequence, the topic has to do with American studies. Initially, Onkere wanted to clearly discuss historical and political ways Dr. Martin Luther King Jr. might have participated in the election of Barack Obama as the forty-fourth US president resulting from the 2008 presidential election. Professor LeGrand expressed concern on such a topic, intellectually arguing it would not have such a tremendous impact because a lot has been already said on Dr. Martin Luther King Jr. Rather, he humbly suggested that Onkere target specific black American political organizations and discuss the role those might have played in the 2008 election of Barack Obama, which he did. In this regard, the former French instructor ended up working on the role some organizations associated with the civil rights movement played in the 2008 election of President Obama. As for the fieldwork and the writing of the dissertation, they would be carried out in America, where the protagonist had returned upon completing his discussion with Professor LeGrand.

DOCTORAL PROGRAM: YEAR 1

Basically, during his first year as a doctoral student, Onkere spent his time at home either reading or writing something related to his dissertation. Whenever he was not doing anything doctorate related, he would take care of his daughter. Indeed, he was in charge of dropping her off and picking her up from school. In the meantime, his fiancée was actually the breadwinner, the one bringing in money to support the family, even though Onkere received some money from his family members, notably his brother Randy. The first year into the doctoral program was a bit painful for Onkere, who until now had been working and bringing money home.

Being the only one working, Onkere's fiancée got tired and frustrated with him. She pressured him to get done with his doctoral studies so they could start living their lives like normal people. She had come to realize that since they met, they had pretty much been holding back living their lives while waiting for something to happen, which seemed not to. By the time he entered the doctoral program, he had been living with his fiancée for almost seven consecutive years. The couple had decided not to have other children anytime soon, not until making sure that they secured their financial future first.

In order to speed up the process for Onkere to make his doctoral defense on time, the former French instructor, his daughter, and fiancée traveled to help him do some fieldwork. They drove from Boston to Chicago. The ride took them a little bit more than three hours. Once in Chicago, he met and talked for about fifteen minutes with one of the most important civil rights leaders in America. Upon informing the latter that he had a meeting set up with the civil rights leader's personal assistant, the leader basically told Onkere that he was in good hands and that his personal assistant was the ideal person to talk to and discuss his organization's role in the struggle for justice and equality in America. While Onkere was talking with the civil rights leader, his daughter kept hiding behind her mother for fear of being touched by the leader. Embarrassed, Onkere's fiancée kept apologizing to the leader, explaining their daughter's attitude. After that encounter, Onkere was taken to the assistant's office, where he actually conducted and recorded a thirty-minute interview granted to him. A big portion of the interview focused on the role played by the said leader by Dr. Martin Luther King Jr.'s side during the civil rights movement. A week following the Chicago trip, the former French instructor and his family visited museums in Cedar Rapids, Iowa, where they actually learned about the 1984 and 1988 presidential runs by the said leader and the impact his runs had on the African American community as well as on the American society as a whole.

While these events were going on, at the same time, back home, Onkere's sister Dah had returned to Mpugu upon successfully completing her doctorate. She was now a professor teaching philosophy at Bonneville University. Yogi, his other sister who had graduated a long time before with a bachelor's degree in sciences, had brilliantly completed a two-year training in another African country. She was working as an air traffic controller at the national airport, while Opy, one of the youngest sisters, was now a second-year doctoral student working toward completing her doctoral dissertation in geography.

As for Onkere's fiancée, Ms. Smith, she had a long time before brilliantly completed a bachelor's degree in psychology from one of the most prestigious universities in America. She had been, therefore, working with mentally challenged kids, a position she had been enjoying. She is a very compassionate human being with remarkable attributes, a person that I have been given the tremendous privilege to know on a personal level. I truly appreciate her friendship, as I consider her as a friend and confidante of mine.

TYING THE KNOT

At this point, if I recall correctly, Onkere and his fiancée were discussing the possibility of tying the knot. The second year into his doctoral program, it was determined that Onkere and his fiancée would move to the next phase of their relationship. Therefore, it was decided that the wedding would take place in June, a day before Onkere's birthday, so that every year he could celebrate two events at the same time. The wedding preparation took almost a year in the making. The wedding was a very important deal for both partners. Onkere would realize nevertheless that it was more like the bride's day than the groom's. Indeed, it really was all about Ms. Smith because, at the end of the day, when the bride is happy and cheerful, apparently so is the husband-to-be and the whole family. For the special occasion, Onkere's family members traveled to America to take part in that very important moment in their brother's life. Given that neither Mister nor his wife could make the trip, Dr. Randy represented both parents. He traveled with his wife. As for Dr. Dah, she attended the wedding with her husband and their newly born son, Jordy. Last but not least, Opy traveled to America. I was there as well to welcome Onkere's family members. On the part of his wife-to-be, people and family members were very active. Her father, Dr. Chuck, had asked one of his friends to officiate the wedding. His wife, the bride's mother, Marggy, an artist and photographer, was very instrumental in making sure that her daughter's wedding was a success, regardless of some disputes and family drama that occurred at different stages leading to the wedding preparation. Many of the misunderstandings and tension were for the most part logistic related. The bride wanted things done a certain way, and that was most likely her way. One of the reasons Onkere liked this moment, apart from the fact that he was going to marry his fiancée, Ms. Smith, the love of his life and mother of his children, was the fact that the whole family stayed at a hotel for about three days. As for the wedding dress code, all the gentlemen were harmoniously dressed in a slightly dark gray color picked by the bride, while all the ladies wore sky-blue dresses.

The bride herself was dressed in a long, homemade white gown featuring elaborate embellishment work on the entire piece, which was not only indicative of a work excellently performed but also of countless hours spent by the designer, handily sewing each piece of the embellishment to give birth to an incredibly gorgeous gown that perfectly suited the bride. The whole work took the designer about three months to complete. Some parts of the dress were also exquisitely and perfectly embroidered. Ms. Smith's appearance in the gown on the day of the wedding was as appealingly breathtaking at first sight as was the dress itself. She just looked ridiculously gorgeous, to the enjoyment of her husband-to-be and certainly the audience attending the wedding ceremony. The ceremonial process and procedures for the wedding had perfectly been rehearsed thousands of times by all the immediate participants in the wedding ceremony. By proceedings, I mean the vows to be exchanged between the bride and the groom, the way they would be facing each other during that process, which lady would precede, moving forward standing behind the bride, or which lady and gentleman go first following the bride's witness. Obviously, the role of the witnesses had clearly been explained and rehearsed countless times so that everything would occur smoothly and accordingly to lessen the bride's stress. Her father had, among other responsibilities, to deal with and handle his daughter's stress. The candlelight process had also carefully been rehearsed, and the family member reading biblical scriptures to bless the couple had already been designated. The rings were already bought, and ring bearers picked. Everything that needed to be done beforehand had already been done, and the ceremony was all the party participants were waiting for.

I remember on the day of the wedding, as if it were yesterday, the attendees standing up while the bride's father, Dr. Chuck, was walking his daughter down the aisle to her husband-to-be. It was an incredibly emotional moment to watch for both families. Once the bride was carefully and smoothly handled to the groom, the ceremony started. The preacher reminded the couple about their marital duties, obligations, and everything they needed to know to successfully remain married. After reminding the couple of their marital duties and prerogatives, he proceeded with asking the couple, the bride first, followed by the groom, to say their vows, which they did. Then, the ring bearers were asked to bring the rings and passed them to the couple's respective witnesses who, in turn, passed them to the couple. Upon receiving the ring, the bride proceeded to insert it on her husband-to-be's left fourth finger, while saying her vows. Once done, the groom went through the same process. It was an amazing and tense, emotional moment to be part of. The remaining parts proceeded as planned. When the part to read biblical scriptures was reached, one of the bride's aunts, Kathleen, read 1 Corinthians 13:4–8 to bless the couple. The scriptures were beautifully read with a remarkable emotional tone. As for the groom's sisters Dr. Dah and Opy, who attended the wedding ceremony, they happened to be Christians by religion. Consequently, they amazingly performed a Christian song, whose title I have forgotten. The whole performance was impressive, particularly because it was excellently carried out in French, a foreign language that the audience attending the wedding was not familiar with. As for Tall, Onkere's confidant, he was his man of honor. He attended the wedding ceremony with his own wife and another friend of his. Sandra, the bride's cousin, was her bridesmaid. She was a bubbly person with short brown hair whose jokes always ended up with her snoring in a weird way. She was fun to be around. At the end of the proceedings following the exchange of rings, the preacher introduced to the audience Mr. and Mrs. Smith Onkere, after declaring them husband and wife.

That night, however, a reception was thrown, and more than four hundred people attended it. Most of them, from Mrs. Smith Onkere's side, were friends of her parents as well as some acquaintances of her own. Onkere's brother Dr. Randy paid a tribute to Mister, while excusing their parents for not attending the wedding. He explained that he had been mandated instead by Mister himself to represent him and his wife at the wedding. The speech, beautifully delivered in French, was excellently translated into English by Tall. It was visibly well received. Among the other personalities who spoke were Dude, Mrs. Smith Onkere's brother, and Dr. Chuck, her father. Both made some well-received jokes, after which the party began. I would be remiss, however, if I did not mention that before Dr. Randy even spoke, Dr. Chuck made an exceptionally outstanding performance by reading his entire speech in French, welcoming his guests as well as his son-in-law's family members. The performance was remarkably executed to the satisfaction of Dr. Randy, who could not help but congratulating Dr. Chuck for his kindly brave gesture. Earlier that afternoon, following the wedding ceremony, the couple and some of their guests toured the city where the wedding was held. Dude was among the group.

Like his sister, Dude holds a bachelor's degree in art and film from one of the most prestigious universities in America. He also was conferred a master's degree in the film industry by another prestigious university. Full of energy, Dude, who has a bubbly personality, dreamed of becoming a movie director someday. I honestly think he can do it. His gentle mania allowed him to kindly bring and distribute big cigars to all the gentlemen of the wedding party. The tour took about three hours, during which pictures were taken in different locations of the city, while champagne was flowing like a river. As for the dances carried out later that night, the father-daughter dance was more than impressive. Mrs. Smith Onkere's father-to-daughter's song was wonderfully performed, after which the former French instructor asked to dance with his wife. They danced to Louis Armstrong's "What a Wonderful World." I still can see the husband singing the song while dancing with his beloved wife.

DOCTORAL FIELDWORK: UNITED STATES OF AMERICA

A week after the euphoria, everything became normal. Onkere's guests returned, and he had to go back to reality. He had to go back to working on his dissertation, given that his wife had been pressuring him to get it done. As a sort of honeymoon, however, he and his wife traveled to some state where they spent three days. The real purpose of the trip was actually to attend an annual conference held by one of the major civil rights organizations in America. While attending the conference, he had the chance to talk with influential members of the organization, given that it was part of his dissertation. During those three days, they met with crucial people from the organization, who basically explained to the couple the role played by its branch divisions and the importance associated with the organization's annual conference. They also were told how pragmatically the organization operates and the process associated with lobbying the American Congress. It was a fascinating learning experience, a thousand times better than learning from books.

Onkere, his wife, children—by now, the couple had welcomed the second and third apples of their eyes, two beautiful daughters named Meely Moo and Sylvers, the baby—and his in-laws also traveled to the South. Meely Moo turned out to be a very bright kid. She is very reserved and well mannered. Her dad has passed down to her his temperament, so much so that she can easily get angry if provoked. However, she is learning how to manage her anxiety and frustrations. She is very protective and loving to her siblings, dad, mom, grandpas, and grandmas. She speaks two international languages as well. Meely Moo loves to swim and play games on her computer. As for Sylvers, she too turned out to be as bright as her older sisters. She is a strong-willed kid who knows what she wants and when she wants it. She has a hard time following instructions. As a result, she gets into trouble with her mom almost all the time. Sylvers loves gymnastics, and it is something she is good at. She does not stop going through her lessons and moves at home. Like both of her sisters, she also speaks two international languages. Sylvers loves her dad, mom, and both of her grandpas and grandmas.

As for the whole family, they went to Tennessee to visit the motel where Dr. King was assassinated on April 4, 1968. They took that opportunity to review some of the events that went down on that day. They revisited the gun as well as the model car James Earl, Dr. Martin Luther King Jr.'s assassin, was driving prior to killing him. While at the motel, Onkere and his wife had a chance to glance at the window from the room Dr. King stayed at prior to that tragic day. Onkere, his wife, and their children also stood on the balcony outside, on the second floor at the motel, right on the very spot Dr.

King was shot. Onkere felt the strong desire to accomplish that kind of ritual or pilgrimage. In order to make every member of our traveling team feel satisfied with the trip, we went to visit Elvis Presley's birthplace and did the Graceland Mansion tour. In that process, we learned the history of the mansion, visited his recording studios, and saw his cars collections and the records and awards he received. Dude, Onkere's brother-in-law, had a blast, given that he is an Elvis Presley fan. That particular tour was his initiative. We all learned something about Elvis Presley we did not know before that trip to Tennessee.

While driving down South, Onkere, his wife, their children, and his in-laws passed through several towns, cities, and states whose sceneries were enjoyably admired. Some of the states and cities we went through were Kansas; Saint Louis, Missouri; Arkansas; and Memphis, Tennessee. We took AI-27 S/State, driving south toward MO-27 S. From there, we took US-62 S, passed through I-64 E, and ended up taking Interstate 55 South to Memphis.

Every time Onkere was given the opportunity to make a trip on the road, he enjoyed it. Driving through some of these states and cities reminded him of a dream he used to have back in Africa. He used to dream that one day he would be in a position allowing him to visit some of the American states and cities he knew and studied when he was a sixth grader, in the early nineties. Onkere had handily designed in different colors a huge and beautiful American map with the fifty states. It hung on the wall in his parents' living room for everyone to see. By the time he graduated from high school, he pretty much knew, out of memory, the majority of American states.

THE INTERVIEWS

Among the professors and scholars that Onkere interviewed as part of his dissertation's fieldwork was Professor X. He actually was teaching some classes at some university at the time. Both as a scholar and personal friend to the main protagonist, Professor X would be among those who were very instrumental in helping our protagonist get the right information, books, and material to smoothly speed up the writing process of his dissertation.

Given that the dissertation discussed the election of Barack Obama, who at the end of the 2008 presidential campaign was elected the forty-fourth US president, the interview with Professor X focused on the notion of a postelection racial America. The professor was also asked to give his views on what the election of the first African American US president meant for America as well as for American politics.

Whenever Onkere needed some explanation for a better understanding of American politics, as also pointed out, he could not find a better critic to seek advice from than the said professor. On the question to know what his views were about the fact that some American politicians were pushing for the idea that one of the candidates running was considered not to be black enough, the said professor basically argued that the reason why that viewpoint came to be had to do with the fact that the said candidate did not grow up in certain neighborhoods. This, in short, relegated him to the status of nonconformity, making it a challenge for his opponents to slot him. It, therefore, made it difficult to battle him on the part of his political opponents, because the said candidate could not be slotted.

To the question relative to what some critics were asserting about the irrelevancy of black political organizations on the grounds that an African American had gotten elected as the US president, the said professor essentially argued about the necessity for those organizations to reassess the purpose of the various groups now that they had achieved one of their goals of breaking through one of the glass ceilings. He went on further arguing that the election of the first African American US president does not mean that equality has occurred. But rather, what that meant was that the political process had become more diverse in America. He contended that the prejudice could always be there as long as human beings exist, because humans are imperfect creatures. He eloquently argued that those organizations did not need to end because their purpose was and, I might add, is still very relevant when it comes to the question of race relations in twenty-first-century America. For the professor, those black political organizations should rejoice in their accomplishment by way of pragmatically reinforcing their efforts of educating masses on how to achieve fairness and equality among all the races. From his standpoint, the election of the first African American US president should, therefore, not be seen as a threat to anyone.

Professor Y was the other scholar whose interview was part of Onkere's doctoral dissertation. As for him, he was asked to give his opinion on how he himself felt when the forty-fourth US president was elected and what the election of the first African American to ever occupy the White House meant for America. To all of these questions, the said professor felt that he was, as the vast majority of Americans, ecstatic when the president was elected.

Frankly, he didn't believe it would happen—not at least in his lifetime. A thousand things could have derailed his campaign. In fact, like many others, the professor even worried about his life, because, to him, America is a country of bewildering extremes. Nevertheless, he was thrilled when the president won. That being said, he believed that America, despite the obvious changes that the president's election symbolized, was hardly a post racial nation. For him, after the election, individuals still caught up in that cathartic and unprecedented moment couldn't see the forest for the trees. And that given the euphoria, they mistakenly thought that the election of the president had heralded a fundamental shift in racial attitudes. But many minorities and subgroups were—and I might add are—still hopelessly trapped in inner-city ghettoes with little hope of escaping. He so eloquently argued that opportunities and chances abound in the United States. But he would articulate that if you were a black child born, for example, when your mother, only fifteen, and your father, a high school dropout, were unemployed, very little about your experience would be post racial. Professor Y's interview was among the latest ones. As such, it actually concluded the interview series. Once the fieldwork was done, Onkere spent the rest of the days and months writing as well as editing his dissertation.

DOCTORAL PROGRAM: YEAR 2

By the end of his second year in the PhD program, he actually got done writing his dissertation, after having made more than six trips back and forth from Pierretteville to America, and vice versa. While in Pierretteville working on his dissertation, his wife and daughter Meely Moo paid him a visit in France. Together, they visited many cities, among which, to name a few, were Limoges, Nancy, and Paris.

During his trips to France, Onkere would sometimes get in touch with a colleague and friend named Spencer. He was not only from Mpugu, but above all, he too, like Onkere, was from Akaga City, the protagonist's place of birth. Onkere would learn later on that he and Spencer were from the same neighborhood back home. Coincidentally, like the former French instructor, Spencer was also working on his doctoral dissertation in the field of English and American civilization. Naturally, their scholarly shared interests for this area reinforced their bonds. Both doctoral students would be of tremendous help to each other till their postdoctoral graduation. On his way back to America, most of the time Onkere would stay at Spencer's place in Paris, where the doctoral students would exchange views on their respective dissertation as well as on current political and economic issues of the day. While Spencer would expand on his research and breaking news in France, Onkere would sometimes update him on breaking news in America pertaining to their field of expertise.

On the American national level, 2012 was an election year. President Barack Obama was seeking a second term. He knew basically that he was going to be the only credible candidate to be nominated on the Democratic side. On the Republican side, former Massachusetts governor Mitt Romney was running.

As expected, he came out winning the Republican primaries and ultimately was the party's nominee for the general election. History has it that Barack Obama won the

2012 presidential election and got reelected for the second time. For Onkere, the reelection of Barack Obama was sufficient proof that the latter had done an excellent job and that he was elected on his own merits, considering the fact that many of his critics falsely argued that his first election was sort of given to him. Onkere paid special attention to that second election as well, particularly to President Obama's campaign, given that part of his doctoral dissertation discusses Obama's 2008 election.

DOCTORAL PROGRAM: YEAR 3

By the third year in the doctoral program, Onkere had written the entire dissertation even though he was still editing it now and then. Given that he was done writing it, he suggested to his dissertation supervisor that the date for the defense be set up. The supervisor nicely rejected the suggestion, arguing that his colleagues, likely to be members of the jury, could have perceived a dissertation written and defended in a three-year period of time as not rigorously and scientifically defendable. Furthermore, he argued, they could likely find multiple irrelevant reasons to discredit such a dissertation.

Upon hearing those arguments, Onkere, who had inherited from his mother patience, endurance, understanding, tolerance, and giving people the benefit of the doubt, cooled off despite the pressure his wife and family members were still putting on him to get his dissertation done \.

Given that he was not allowed to make his defense in that third year, Onkere had no other choice than to travel back to America, where he would just be waiting for the defense's date to be set up. In the meantime, while waiting for the PhD defense, the protagonist was accepted as an instructor of English and communication at Eliriga University, one of the top ten universities in America, for one academic year. The contract, he was told, could be extended if need be. Yet, upon getting his PhD, as would be discussed, he had to return to his country of origin.

ELIRIGA UNIVERSITY: ENGLISH INSTRUCTOR

I was assigned three classes. All three of them were sophomore classes. In the first two, I taught English Level 2, and I taught principles of communication to the third class. I taught four days out of five and had classes on Mondays, Wednesdays, Thursdays, and Fridays. As for the classes, English Level 2 consisted of teaching students not only English grammatical rules but also how to write papers and the elements that help in punctuating scholarly written papers. Teaching that course helped me improve my own knowledge while revisiting some elements I might have forgotten when it came to writing dissertations, given that I actually was still editing my own doctoral thesis.

As for the principles of communication class, one of the key elements that the students were supposed to learn and understand was the way gestures, meanings, and interpretation of nonverbal communication could be different from one culture to another or from one country to another.

Together, the students and I went over those details and reviewed both the importance of verbal and nonverbal communication. Another element in this particular course was the ability of students to orally express themselves. Teaching this class reminded me of how far I had come from my days back in Toshville as a high school student, as well as a freshman from the English department where I once was judged on my ability to orally perform. I saw myself teaching students good manners and public-speaking lessons to become successful and excellent communicators.

Students were required to make speeches they would have elaborated themselves by telling their own stories, clearly, after I initially taught them the different types of speeches there are to know as well as the purpose of each of them. The students enjoyed this course as much as I liked it. The students were made up of different backgrounds and ethnicities: whites, blacks, Asians, and Latinos. Surprisingly enough, I had two African black students in my class, a young man and a young girl. As for my course supervisor, he was a very nice and understanding associate professor of English for whom I had tremendous respect. He was a very open-minded gentleman who treated me as an equal even though I knew what my place was. I would seek any teaching-related advice from him, and whenever I had an issue, I would consult with him. We basically shared the same office, divided into two parts by an artificial movable wall. All I needed to do was stand up to see whether or not he was in his office, and vice versa. All in all, I had a great and wonderful time teaching at Eliriga University, even though I was still working and thinking about getting done with defending my own PhD dissertation.

THE DOCTORAL DEFENSE

During fall of the following year, more than fifteen years after Onkere first came across the English language, he successfully defended his doctoral dissertation in the presence of his brother Dr. Randy, his sister Opy, and the audience composed of some apprehensive doctoral students.

Onkere's wife could not attend the defense, given that by then she was taking care of the kids. As already pointed out, their second and third daughters, Meely Moo and Sylvers, had already been born. At the end of a brilliantly performed defense that went on for over four straight hours, Onkere was officially conferred the title of doctor in the field of English and American civilization. He was worn out, yet incredibly delighted, as was everybody else in the room. Dr. Patty and Dr. Ismael, two former graduates from Pierrette University who attended the defense ceremony, were very instrumental in helping Onkere grasp the way the academic system worked within Pierrette University. Both doctors showed Dr. Onkere how to maneuver within the system. Dr. Onkere learned a great deal from both of these remarkable individuals full of love, compassion, and understanding. They were very supportive of Dr. Onkere's efforts to fit in.

On that day, Dr. Onkere, who was most likely overwhelmed with everything that had transpired, thought about his parents, Mister, his mother, brothers, and sisters. He more specifically thought about Fefe, the Joneses, Professor Pitcherson, his wife, Mrs. Smith Onkere, their children, his in-laws, and everyone else who had contributed to making him become who he had become by securing a doctorate in the field of English, a language he had fallen in love with, at first sight, almost two decades ago. Along the way, regardless of the many obstacles he came across, Dr. Onkere never gave up his dream and kept pushing toward realizing it. By being conferred a doctorate in the field of English and American civilization, he had proven to himself how far he had come to master not only the language but also part of a civilization of the people whose language is English.

There is, in the final analysis, the mastering of a culture from a civilization point of view and the fact that the said culture could now be explained in the language whose people belonging to it express themselves with. The point is that Dr. Onkere had acquired not just one element—the English language—but a second aspect, which is his capacity to express himself in such areas as American politics, American studies, American sociology, or the American civil rights movement, considering that his interdisciplinary doctoral dissertation covered all of these areas. Apart from the language itself, he has the intellectual authority bestowed upon him when conferred his doctorate. The degree conferred qualifies him as a doctor of English and also as a doctor of American civilization. In a sense, it is like him having killed two birds with one stone. This is one of the many specificities associated with the doctorate conferred to him. The next day following the defense, Dr. Onkere flew right back to America to be with his wife and children and to enjoy the completion of his studies in English, a journey started almost two decades before. Dr. Onkere was now an expert in the field of English and American civilization, and that was no small accomplishment at all, to say the least. I know that he was proud of himself, especially after everything he went through to accomplish what he had accomplished: all the ridiculous setbacks during the course of his studies, the requirements imposed on him, the unnecessary misunderstandings with students and supervisors, the negative criticism and questions about his intellectual abilities and capacities, the sleepless nights, the moves and change of residencies through cities, countries, and continents, the challenges he had to take on to move ahead with his studies, and all the unforeseen tricks he overcame. None of these exogenous factors could prevent him from succeeding. The road toward success was not that easy for him. However, he ended up prevailing because he had stubbornly aimed high. While attending his brother's doctoral defense, Dr. Randy reminded him of the urgency to return home, given that Dr. Onkere had promised his father, Mister, that he would return home upon completing his studies, which he just did. Consequently, upon returning to America, he and his wife kept discussing the possibility of them moving to Mpugu, a discussion they had already had many times.

In order to get straight to work once in Mpugu, Dr. Onkere was approached by Dr. Spencer, his friend who had successfully been conferred a doctorate in the field of English and American civilization about six months prior to Dr. Onkere being conferred his. Dr. Spencer had actually been teaching at Bonneville University for some time while working on completing his doctoral dissertation. Upon receiving his PhD, he went back home right away to upgrade his status to that of assistant professor of English and American studies. Knowing Dr. Onkere's academic background, Dr. Spencer suggested to the head of the English department that he knew of a young scholar who was living in America who had just been conferred a doctorate in the field of American studies. Upon agreeing on reviewing his dossier, Dr. Onkere was contacted by Dr. Spencer to submit an application file, which he did. Two weeks later, Dr. Dave, the head of the English department, gave Dr. Onkere a call, advising him that his application had been reviewed by a committee and that a vote had unanimously been passed in his favor, and he had been accepted as a new member of the English department. Upon receiving the good news, Dr. Onkere shared it with his wife. Going forward, for the remaining months prior to their departure to Mpugu, the couple spent time figuring things out regarding accommodations and the like. During the following months, it was decided that Dr. Onkere would precede his wife and their children to make sure that when the family joined him in Mpugu, the transition would go smoothly, especially given that Sylvers, the third daughter to the couple, was still a baby. As such, she still needed special attention and care.

CHAPTER 9

Returning Home: Africa

Returning home upon completing the course
of one's studies abroad is an imperative.
—Onanga Raymond

BONNEVILLE: THE CAPITAL CITY

After spending more than a decade abroad, I am positive that Dr. Onkere knew the transition—returning home—was not going to be a piece of cake. But given that there is no place like home, he had the moral obligation to return, honoring the promise he made to his father, Mister. The capacity for individuals to honor their promises says a lot about their personality, something Dr. Onkere knew. Prior to getting on board the flight taking him back home, he had informed close relatives of his arrival. Indeed, once the flight landed the next day at Bonneville's international airport, his family members were there to give him a big African welcome. Pretty much everyone was there: his sisters, cousins, nieces, nephews, and little brother. From the airport, they went straight up to Dr. Dah's place, where he spent the night. The next day, he went to see Mister and his mother, who both were living at their place. There, he hung out with the family members who came to greet him. Olivia and Mariella also came to see their brother. Mister was as much overjoyed as was his wife, Tessina Monray. By the third day of staying at his sister's place, Dr. Onkere, who had already anticipated the kind of neighborhood he wanted his family to reside in, started looking for a house there. He found it and moved in the following day. The house was a kind of duplex with the landlord residing on the top level, while Dr. Onkere and his family would occupy the apartment located on the inferior level. It was a white house nicely built, with a fence and a garage in which more than three cars could easily be parked. While living by himself prior to the arrival of his wife and children, Dr. Onkere did the best he could to make the residence look very nice. Also, prior to his arrival, he had already scheduled an appointment with Dr. Spencer to discuss and go over his appointment to the university.

A week after he got back home, Dr. Onkere was more than excited to pay the head of the English department a visit to inquire about the process moving forward and what needed to be done to process the paperwork. During the meeting that ensued, the head of the English department, Dr. Dave, provided him with all the necessary information. From there, he went to the secretariat general of the university and filled out all the administrative documents relative to his new teaching position, after which he officially became assistant professor of English and American civilization. He then went back to talk with the head of the department,

Dr. Dave, a very understanding and humble gentleman who gave him the schedule and assigned him three classes. Two of them were freshman classes. The third one was a sophomore class. He was scheduled to teach two days out of five, on Tuesdays and Fridays.

BONNEVILLE UNIVERSITY: YEAR 1

In one of the freshman classes, he taught oral expression and phonetics, while in the other one, he would teach applied English. During his first year at the university, he taught a course on American politics as applied English.

The texts studied focused mainly on the American political system and ideologies. One of the main objectives of that course was the professor's willingness and intent to solidly help build his students' vocabulary and terminology in the field of American politics. To do that, the professor used many of the materials he himself had used while completing his doctoral dissertation, part of which was on American politics. He had acquired, therefore, what it took to teach that course. He also loved American politics, for having made intense research on the topic. As for the sophomore level, he would normally teach a course on American civilization. I need to mention that out of all the professors from the department, only three specialized in American civilization. These three professors were in charge of not only administering this subject but also helping redesign its curriculum. Professor Onkere was one of them.

While teaching at the English department where he himself once attended as a student, Professor Onkere was amazingly surprised to find out that some of the professors who taught him English were still there. Nevertheless, regardless of the fact that he now was officially their colleague, he had a hard time considering them as such. It was strange for him to even start accepting that they were on the same intellectual level, at least when it came to the degree that allowed all of them to be teaching at the university. Still, he had deferent respect toward them. Surprisingly enough for some of them, he would address them as "Professor," "Sir," or "Madame." Whenever he did that in front of his own students, they would ask him why he was not addressing his colleagues by their last or first names. To that, he would always answer saying that he once was a student there, where his own students were standing right there. He would argue that they taught him English, and he addressed them that way for more than three years of his existence. It sounded weird for him, therefore, to address them otherwise. Plus, as Africans and a Bantu people, the elders must be respected. He owed them that respect. By nature, Professor Onkere has his father's personality. In order to avoid getting misunderstood while growing up, he gradually had to learn, like his father, to seriously hide and repress a certain attitude by cherishing values such as always treating people in a decent manner no matter who they are, being very respectful of the elders, and always making sure, in any circumstance, to be on the right side of justice. Practicing this sort of living philosophy had profoundly humbled our main protagonist by radically changing who he once was. Professor Onkere, for obvious reasons, was excited to be teaching English and American civilization to what— from a strictly African cultural standpoint—he considered as his little brothers and sisters. But in reality, they were his students. As such, they were not blood relatives of his. He was energized, full of passion, and eagerly motivated to serve and share his knowledge and acquired experiences with them. I can assure you that his little brothers and sisters appreciated him as much as he appreciated them.

In his Oral Expression class, Professor Onkere felt the moral obligation to take his own materials, laptop and loudspeakers, to properly conduct listening sessions. The truth is that he had already gotten the pedagogical material and tools needed to conduct such a course. His little brothers and sisters greatly appreciated him bringing his own material during his different sessions. What Professor Onkere was doing was also part of his own teaching philosophy, which will clearly be alluded to later on, a philosophy he had used primarily teaching in American university institutions. Given that one of the Oral Expression course's main objectives was to build students' confidence and efficiency in their ability to orally express themselves in English, Professor Onkere would pick topics relative to the American civilization or culture and ask students to pick the ones they wanted to make their oral presentations on. He would then put them into groups of no more than ten students for them to efficiently teamwork so as to confidently present their findings to the whole class. The assignment was twofold. It was aimed to allow them to start doing research on their own. On the other hand, the purpose was to give them the chance to come and orally present it to the class, showing everybody how well and easily they could express themselves in English—the core objective of the course being taught. Sometimes Professor Onkere would help by giving very specific orientations to the students. Most of the time, he would do it if approached by students with questions. In his phonetics course, things went also very smoothly. Prior to returning home, while still being abroad, he had purchased many books dealing with phonetics and pronunciation. And so he was ready to venture into that domain. Here again, he would use his own material because, on top of the translation and transcription, he also had listening sessions with his little brothers and sisters. The majority of the listening done was from different sources and material. They were obtained from speeches by some American famous personalities and politicians. They also came from audio books or tapes. Additionally, audio CDs on pronunciation were also worked on. During all the sessions, Professor Onkere made sure that courses were understood by his students. He would consequently pick the extracts where he knew the vocabulary had been covered. The listening parts would take sometimes five to ten minutes, after which the professor would distribute a questionnaire to the class. He would then play again the CD and ask students to answer the questions. That was done during a training session. The tests followed pretty much the same process.

Prior to teaching any class, on the very first day, in all his three classes, Professor Onkere was very honest with his students. He told them that he was very open-minded, that he was there to help them and facilitate their learning process. He furthermore made it clear that he believed in meritocracy. As a consequence, he reminded his little brothers and sisters that grades would imperatively and only be allocated on merit and that no negotiation whatsoever would be allowed.

He went on, explaining that he was willing and able to help before, during, or after class with lessons or courses not well understood. He was willing and able even to lend books, provided they be returned to him on due time.

Coming from America and having taught for several academic years at Charles-Raymond University where, before every school year, together with his colleagues, he underwent pedagogic trainings, Professor Onkere knew full well what his duties and responsibilities were while teaching at Bonneville University. Not only that, like in Charles-Raymond University, or Eliriga University where he also taught English, he was fully aware of the harassment issue going on at the university level. Therefore, head-on, he addressed it by reminding all his students that he was happily married and that he would not tolerate any misunderstanding on that issue. I can tell that students respected him more because of his honesty and openness. I strongly believe that the many training sessions he went through in America served him well during the years he spent teaching at Bonneville University.

There is no doubt in my mind that Professor Onkere was really proud to be teaching at the university, for having been himself a student at the same university. More specifically, he enjoyed passionately teaching his American Civilization course. The beauty of that class was that he liked the curriculum that was being taught at the sophomore level. It specifically dealt with issues of racial identity, race, gender study, American government, American Civil War, the civil rights movement, and American political parties and ideologies. In short, part of the curriculum discussed some of the issues and approaches he used in the doctoral dissertation he had just completed.

What this means is that he beautifully had grasped beyond comprehension these issues and had them at the tip of his fingers. He simply loved it. He had watched and even visited certain spots and locations where some of the events specifically related to the civil rights movement took place. He was still living in America while the first African American US president got elected for the first and second consecutive time. This means that he had witnessed with particular attention how American political parties and ideologies played out during presidential elections. More interestingly enough, all his experiences while researching data relative to his dissertation, as well as traveling American towns, cities, and states, had given him plenty of knowledge to teach American courses without needing to stick to his notes or remarks while teaching them. Instead, Professor Onkere would come to class and simply discuss the events as well as their historicity as if he were there, present on the spots when they actually happened. The students themselves were very engaging and challenging, and Professor Onkere liked that spirit. It motivated him, even more, to be teaching there. He knew he had to be up to the task, and I believe he was considering the feedback he received from his little brothers and sisters attending his classes.

Professor Onkere's teaching philosophy, to speak of it, consisted of making sure that the students understood the material. At the very beginning of the school year, he would dispatch, in advance, hard copies of all the lessons to be carefully and methodically examined, discussed, and reviewed during the course of the year. As such, it gave students plenty of time to go over the material before they came to classes. After each lesson, he would announce what the next one would be and ask students to review it so as to bring questions during the next session. He figured that by having lessons in advance, students would be able to follow him while teaching and explaining them. This, in his case, was basically teaching out of memory.

Part of his teaching style was to come in class and ask students if they had questions on the lesson studied or if they understood the whole previous lesson. In case no hand was raised, students would be asked to read the material. Occasionally, he would read it himself. Once the reading was over, he would then get into explaining the lesson out of memory. This process always and ultimately resulted in students asking lots of questions, taking notes, and him emphasizing points students might not have understood. Those courses were most of the time well and passionately taught, to the degree that he did not have to ask his little brothers and sisters to pay attention because they were into the course being taught. Professor Onkere always taught that specific American Civilization class with passion. He always felt energized while teaching it. It was obvious to his students that he just had fun teaching that class. Professor Onkere's teaching method was amazing to watch, partly because of the way he spoke, pronounced, and expressed himself. While many students appreciated the way he sounded, some, especially freshmen, had real trouble understanding his Americanized accent.

THE COMPLAINT

Three to five months into teaching, Professor Dave, the head of the department, whom Professor Onkere had by now become close to, summoned the latter to his office. Once there, after chatting a little bit, he was told that a group of students—he was never told their level—had gone to see the head of the department and complained about the fact that they were having issues understanding his Americanized English accent.

Basically, they complained that, contrary to his colleagues whom they had no problem understanding, most of the time they could not get what Professor Onkere was saying because they were not accustomed to his diction.

The head of the department made it clear that he sided with me and explained to the group of students that they actually were fortunate to have an experienced professor like me who had taught both French and English at different American universities for several academic years. Professor Dave also explained to that same group of students that it was fitting I sounded the way I did. That being said, the head of the department asked me nevertheless to remember that the majority of the students were not fluent in English and that many of them might have registered in the department because they had no other choice. Later that day, once back to my place, I thought about the misunderstanding with the students from my morning class while I was teaching at an American university. Many of those students picked my class as a requirement—not because they loved the subject. I got into some sort of trouble because they felt I was being harsh on them. Similarly, I figured the head of the department could be right.

To make sure that he would make the appropriate decision, Professor Onkere also went to his sister Professor Dah, who had been teaching philosophy at the same university, so she could provide him with some insights. He explained to her what had happened. Upon hearing the issue, she sat with Professor Dave. She cautiously advised her brother to speak in such a way that students would understand him. She asked him to use French while explaining or clarifying misunderstood points of the lessons. Given that Mpugu is a French-speaking country, she argued that regardless of the fact that her brother was teaching English and American studies, he still could use French to explain unclear parts of the lesson to help students have the same level of information. She also told her brother that, at the end of the day, the purpose of teaching is to make it so that the students get the best of it by understanding the material being taught. If the students do not understand it, then it could likely be said that the professor teaching the subject in question, she argued, was not academically qualified to teach it. Basically, Professor Dah was suggesting that if students kept complaining, in the final analysis, Professor Onkere could likely be blamed for it.

Professor Onkere, who took valuable pedagogy classes from some American university, entitled Principles of Teaching Foreign Languages, on top of all the training sessions he underwent, knew full well that he had to soften his teaching approach by using a bit of French in the spirit of clarifying things for those of his students who could not comprehend explanations given in English. During the next circle of classes, he indeed softened his approach. He explained to his students the reasons for doing so.

Despite the complaint brought to the attention of the head of the department—and not to the instructor's himself—Professor Onkere never experienced any hostility or in-your-face type of attitude from any of his students. The atmosphere with them remained a peaceful one the entire time. His students looked up to him for different kinds of advice, either school related or occasionally personal. Some of them would come to him just so they could practice English, while others would go to him and ask how and what he did to become professor of English and American civilization, expressing himself as beautifully as he was doing. Some students would just go asking him what he did to become who he was—whatever that might even mean. In all honesty, what some, if not the majority of the students, could not bluntly say to him was that he was an accomplished professor who had traveled parts of the world, exchanged and confronted his knowledge with that of other accomplished professors, personalities of all sorts and backgrounds, and studied and lived in Africa, Europe, and America—three continents from which he ended up being conferred university degrees. Furthermore, they were implying that on top of having been conferred degrees, he had worked and taught at different university levels in Europe and especially in America. They definitely were suggesting that he was a doctor, teaching them English and American studies. The students were also underlying the mere fact that he was married to one of the most beautiful ladies, representing the perfect picture God created, ranking in the second position after the professor's own mother, whom he loves dearly. His wife, to speak of her, clearly knew how he felt about his mother. Still, despite all these factors and attributes, he remained a very humble gentleman who respected and treated students with dignity. He never bragged about his accomplishments—whatever they might be. The reality is that Professor Onkere had been inspired by his students. Ultimately, after interviewing the protagonist for more than a month, while recording every little detail of his story and his many experiences as a professor, I actually decided to write and share his story with the public, partially as a way to answer some of the numerous questions his students from Europe, America, and Africa in particular could not stop asking him about how he came to love the English language.

WIFE AND CHILDREN'S ARRIVAL

On the family and personal levels, about six months after Professor Onkere left America, his wife and children joined him in Africa. Their oldest child remained in America to finish her high school curriculum. She was scheduled to visit them during the next Christmas and New Year. Needless to say, Professor Onkere was more than cheerful and delighted to welcome his wife and children to his home country. The rest of his family was delighted as well.

In fact, on the day of their arrival, he was accompanied by his sisters Djoka, Eyila, and Dr. Dah and some of his nieces and nephews. From the airport, the whole family went straight to his place, where things were set up to warmly welcome them. It would take his wife less than a week to figure things out around the house and find her way to where everything was located.

Less than two weeks of her being back in Bonneville, Professor Onkere took his wife for a special ride through the city. The purpose was to actually educate her on how to drive a car in Bonneville —something she did not learn to do while previously living there— what to do and what not to do, given that taxi men, for the most part, did not follow driving directions, regulations, or laws. For instance, there are fundamental driving rules that require all drivers to remain on the right lane of the road. Taxi drivers do not respect that rule. Therefore, they make it hard for other drivers to smoothly go around them. To avoid any tailgating, it becomes necessary for drivers not used to driving in the capital city to constantly remain, unfortunately, in the left passing lane. Considering that Mrs. Smith Onkere would eventually be driving by herself, she had to know all of these tricks. Professor Onkere did a positive action by taking his wife to experience that drive. A day after that ride, his wife took him for a special drive too, to practice what she had learned the previous day. I can safely report that she did a wonderful job out there on the road. Her husband had, in the meantime, enrolled her in a center where she started to seriously learn the French language. The children would also be enrolled in private kindergartens. After the family joined Professor Onkere, everything worked out perfectly, as planned.

THE CULTURAL SHOCK

Mrs. Smith Onkere was shocked in the beginning because the city had changed since she left almost a decade ago. Gradually, she readjusted very well. She, later on, would tell her husband, once back in America, how she loved and enjoyed living again in Africa. Professor Onkere was impressed by the rapid and exceptional ability of his beautiful wife as she grasped the French language. As of now, she has become an expert in speaking the French language. She exhibits that French je ne sais quoi type of attitude whenever she expresses herself in this language. The protagonist always has a blast every time he observes his wife and older daughter going at it, challenging each other on who best speaks French.

The children had fun too. They enjoyed living in Africa as well. Africa, the land of their father, their land. They socialized with their cousins, as kids do. The time they spent attending kindergartens and playing with their relatives helped a great deal in them learning and speaking French, as kids of their age easily would. Their father was actually impressed with their amazing ability to learn and progress in French. Meely Moo, in particular, was fluent in French because she practiced it the most while playing with her cousins Jordy and Shaly, Dr. Dah's children. Sylvers, the youngest, also picked up some French words and spoke the language as would a three-year-old little girl. Both kids had acquired more than the basics that allowed them to get and say what they needed in the French language. And for that, their dad could not have been happier.

As promised, Stinky Peedles, the protagonist's oldest daughter, would visit Africa during the following spring break. She actually came to visit and traveled with both of her grandparents, Marggy and Dr. Chuck, Mrs. Smith Onkere's parents. Stinky Peedles was fluent in French. She had been taking it since high school and would most of the time work with her daddy so as to improve her understanding of the language. While in Bonneville, Professor Onkere and his wife organized an African safari tour, during which Marggy, the photographer-artist took very nice pictures of sceneries and wild animals such as elephants and rhinoceros. Prior to that safari tour, Professor Onkere's in-laws had the opportunity to meet with Mister and Mrs. Tassina Monray. The meeting was a special moment for the main protagonist in the sense that he had to translate conversations from English to French and vice versa to facilitate the communication between his parents and his in-laws. More importantly, he felt delighted that the latter got a chance to actually meet his parents and especially Mister, his father. All in all, Professor Onkere's in-laws, I can only assume, had a great time visiting Africa, especially Bonneville.

In the meantime, Professor Onkere was appointed as an adviser to the international relations department. This meant that he had to work both at the university and in the above-mentioned department. In his capacity as an adviser, he would occasionally travel abroad. While these events were occurring, on the national and domestic levels, Mpugu was gearing toward a presidential election.

PRESIDENTIAL ELECTION

Political parties were all getting excited. All over the country, political rallies and meetings had already begun. By this time, Dr. Randy, the protagonist's brother, had completed his ambassadorial tenure and had already returned to Mpugu, where he was now a politician working nationally and locally on behalf of his candidate, Nganstie.

In order to help his brother campaigning, citizen Onkere would travel with his brother's political team to their electoral constituency.

While those trips were going on, Professor Onkere never missed any class. He kept teaching, sharing his experience and knowledge with his little brothers and sisters. As for the first academic year, it ended smoothly. The last day of class, grades were calculated with students present so things were clear for everyone. Once everybody agreed on their grades, results were submitted to the head of the department. Grades submission signified the starting point of summer break, which also coincided with Mrs. Smith Onkere traveling back to America to take care of personal business.

MRS. SMITH ONKERE RETURNING TO AMERICA

Given that Professor Onkere was gone most of the time for either professional or political reasons, and considering that his wife, by this time of the year, had urgent needs, and not knowing what the political outcome would be following the presidential election results, Mrs. Smith Onkere's husband figured it was necessary for his wife and children to return to America.

The husband, in the meantime, remained to campaign, teaching and taking care of international relations. In his capacity as an adviser, Professor Onkere normally would use the English language as a working tool whenever the department dealt with international organizations. He would be part of Mpugu's delegation during any kind of negotiation or initiative. On top of that, he would get in touch with Mpugu's counterpart whenever his immediate boss had to attend conferences overseas. Ultimately, he would, in most cases, be part of those trips.

Professor Onkere knew himself that one of the fundamental reasons he had been picked for that position was his capacity, ability, and fluency in expressing himself in English, together with the fact that he knew a lot about the Anglo-Saxon world. He had more than once been an international student, studying and living first in Europe and then in America. On top of this, he had been teaching applied English at the university, focusing on American politics and government. Prior to his appointment, Professor Onkere had been teaching not only political but also economic English. He was thus more familiar with economic and political terminologies and concepts. He was aware of international organizations such as the International Monetary Fund (IMF), United Nations Educational, Scientific, and Cultural Organization (UNESCO), and the United Nations, where financial and diplomatic issues are discussed most of the time using not only French but above all English. The latter language is a plus during official meetings and conferences.

THE PARIS MISSION

Adviser Onkere traveled numerous times overseas, and notably to Paris where he attended a conference on sustainable development, thus representing his boss and the entire department of international relations. While some debates and discussions were carried out in French, most of the speeches were delivered in English.

During that conference, English became necessary for the French-speaking adviser, who could understand and speak the language in question.

The Paris trip was really a game changer, as well as an eye-opener for Adviser Onkere. It also was an eye-opener for me, as I was part of the trip. Once in Paris, Adviser Onkere and I made sure that we booked our hotel rooms as near as possible to the location where the conference would be taking place. By doing this, our intent was to unquestionably make certain we would do the job for which we had been assigned. We would definitely be attending all the meetings, conferences, and any side event linked with the main conference. We booked a hotel that was a six-minute walk from the headquarters, about two blocks away from the conference venue.

Some of our colleagues found accommodations far away from the headquarters. The rationale was that the farther away from the venue, the less expansive it would be. By doing this, some colleagues undoubtedly saved money. Even though that theory happened to be true, it, unfortunately, had a negative impact on their performance and representation, or lack thereof, during the debates. They would show up late, almost by the time discussions were over. Some other times, they would not show up at all. Adviser Onkere and I would attend debates on their behalf, because we did not want to leave seats assigned to our country empty. Strangely enough, the money our colleagues saved up allowed them, on the way back home, to purchase clothes and luxury material. Once back home, a report was made to the boss, detailing what we had accomplished while attending the Paris conference. I certainly understood Adviser Onkere's disappointment. It was absolutely not that his colleagues did some shopping. His irritability was rather due to the fact that they fought their hearts out just to be part of the Paris trip and got paid to do a job they ended up not doing well, if at all.

They chose not to attend discussions and debates as much as they should have. Adviser Onkere's work ethic just could not tolerate such behavior on their part. In all honesty, he himself did some shopping as well. But he, first and foremost, did the job that the Paris trip was designed for. The kind of unprofessional attitude exhibited by some of his colleagues, he argued, inevitably contributed to keeping some African countries underdeveloped. Adviser Onkere and I realized that this trend has regrettably been going on, and it was a sad and shocking reality to both of us.

BONNEVILLE UNIVERSITY: YEAR 2

As for the university, the following year, Professor Onkere kept teaching almost the same classes and lessons, though presented from new perspectives. There were some new faces and old ones in the three classes he was assigned to. He clearly laid out his teaching philosophy by making clear what he expected from his students and how he would make things easy for them to comprehend.

Like Professor Onkere, I had my own teaching philosophy. In fact, believe it or not, I happen to be an instructor myself. To me, teaching is all about sharing my knowledge with students. This is primarily done by encouraging them to participate in class activities. It is also done by setting goals and giving students academic tools that will ultimately help them develop and mature. Interacting with students in such a way that encourages them to ask me as many questions as possible is important to me.

One way of checking if the material taught is learned is by testing students. On top of home assignments, I also like oral questioning. In fact, oral quizzing teaches students to become quick thinkers while helping them express themselves by way of building their confidence on the topic being discussed. Depending on what the feedback is, I would normally adjust or reinforce lessons. In this regard, I apply behaviorism as a teaching and learning method whenever necessary. A practical way to helping students learn is by putting them in small groups of three to six people. The number varies according to the size of the class. Teaming up students allows them to interact with one another. This creates a very good learning environment where those who understand better the course help out the ones who seem to have difficulty grasping the issues. I like to listen to what they have to say to me during these sessions. As an instructor, I always do my best to make the classroom an environment where all opinions are welcomed and respected; a setting where students and I, or students among themselves can disagree without being disagreeable. I strongly believe that diversity, cultural differences, and racial groups need to be taken into account for any instructor to be successful. Teaching in such environments as American, French, and African universities allowed me to be very open-minded to accepting and recognizing that there are different views out there that must be respected. The majority of my students have always considered me as a role model. Also, as an instructor, I like to serve as a sort of motivational speaker. As such, teaching for me comes also down to sharing my own educational background, my own story and teaching experiences in order to motivate students to learn and understand the positive impact they can make on the world through education. And, so far, that part of my teaching has always been very well received and appreciated by students. Naturally, I like to intellectually challenge students, and I welcome them to challenge me back. This, however, must be done in a very nice and polite way.

The objective is to bring students to realize areas they and I respectively need to work on. Honesty is important to me as a professor. When I started teaching, if asked questions whose answers I did not know or had forgotten, I would honestly tell students that I would look into it and provide them with the right answers the next time around. This practice has always served me right. By doing this, one of my objectives was and will always be to show students that, as a professor, I am still a human being with limits. Moreover, I also wanted and will always want to point out that it is okay not to have answers right away about everything but that we should always research them. This teaching perspective of mine relies upon Socrates's learning theory, which basically says that knowledge starts with the recognition of our ignorance and that the realization of that ignorance allows us to research what we did not know in order to know it. Finally, I took a graduate seminar class on the principles of teaching and learning foreign languages. That seminar was all about teaching philosophies and learning methodologies. I learned that there are different learning styles and that for an instructor to be successful, these styles need to be accommodated accordingly. That is why, on top of the traditional tools used to teach, I also use technology, showcase films, visualize documents, watch documentaries, and use YouTube videos and the internet as teaching materials.

As for Professor Onkere's teaching philosophy, it was privately discussed with his own students, and they understood and appreciated their professor's honesty. By privately sharing his teaching philosophy with his little brothers and sisters, Professor Onkere hoped to bring them to open up and realize that he was there to help and not prevent them from realizing their potential as some professors, a decade ago, would do. In fact, in some African universities, it is almost a crime for a professor to give, for example, a score of twenty out of twenty to students. If that happens to be the case, the professor in question could have some explanations to make, to the head of the department or even the president of the university. Even among colleagues, there are those who would strongly discourage their peers, asking them not to give A+ to students. Professor Onkere was not one of them, and students greatly appreciated him for exhibiting some credibility. He had given A+ as well a score of eighteen out of twenty to some of his students when they deserved these grades.

THE MOTIVATIONAL SPEAKER

On top of teaching, Professor Onkere became a sort of motivational speaker to his little brothers and sisters. Given that many of them appreciated his teachings, they had unconsciously put him on a kind of pedestal. Therefore, he wanted to set the record straight by encouraging them to come to the understanding that what he had accomplished as a scholar was not impossible or out of reach for them to achieve. Rather, it was possible for every one of them. He firmly believed that his students could be well trained in English and become as fluent as he was. In order to get where he was, he would argue, they needed, however, to be determined, focused, and resilient and work as hard as they could. Furthermore, he would, in a brotherly manner, explain to them that obtaining a doctorate was not the end but one of the means that would allow them to accomplish great things in life. He also would genuinely tell his little brothers and sisters that they needed to be very open-minded and understanding, while being willing to accept criticism and view it as a tool that would inevitably help them grow. He also would encourage the ladies and gentlemen attending his classes to listen to music in English and read as many books as they possibly could. He would also sometimes ask them to practice speaking the language in front of a mirror whenever possible to ultimately become fluent in English.

He would some other time vehemently address the fact that when he was a freshman or sophomore, there pretty much was no YouTube, internet, or cable television where one could watch any documentary in English. Yet, regardless of that reality, he had succeeded and was standing in front of them. He, above all, would honestly argue that the primary job for his little brothers and sisters was to study, by any means necessary, quoting, of course, Malcolm X.

ETHNICITY STEREOTYPING

I strongly believe that Professor Onkere's open-mindedness, brilliance, reserved attitude, and willingness to take time to talk with his students, on top of his outstanding ability and teaching style, made the majority of them wonder if he really was from Akaga City. One day, in fact, coming out of his American civilization course with sophomore students, out of the blue, a group of students came to him. After respectfully greeting him with some palpable hesitation, they took the courage to finally ask him some questions.

"Sir, we heard that you are from Akaga City. Is that right, sir?"

Pretending that he did not grasp what the student just said, Professor Onkere asked the student to repeat himself.

"Sir, Professor Spencer told us that you are from the Haute-Savana province, and we just could not believe it given your mastering of American topics, your fluency, and efficiency in English. It's impressive."

Upon hearing this, Professor Onkere asked where these students of his were from. "We all are from the Haute-Savana province, sir!"

To that answer, and in order to be sure, Professor Onkere asked his students whether they could tell him, in any language spoken from there, what their names were—which all of them did.

On that note, Professor Onkere affirmatively and positively answered their questions, crediting Professor Spencer's accuracy about his origin and place of birth.

Upon answering their questions, one of the students pointed out how unbelievable this was and how, while attending my lectures, he would have goose bumps not just hearing me speak English but, above all, watching how incredibly knowledgeable I was. All of them, right there, showed a sense of pride, a sense of relief, a sense of having accomplished something through me, through my existence, through the simple fact of my being there, standing in front of them as a professor of English and American studies. I felt incredibly overwhelmed while they were gleefully beaming with pleasure. They enthusiastically felt that change really was in the air in Mpugu and that a new generation of outstandingly, unquestionably, and highly inclined intellectual young men and women from Haute-Savana was emerging and that I was just one of them. They reminded me that not long ago, people whose origin was from where all of them came were wrongly considered or perceived to be less intelligent at accomplishing anything intellectually related, let alone impeccably speaking a foreign language. I had to get political, a little bit. Of course, I undoubtedly did not buy that assertion even though I had heard that subjectively motivated, preconceived idea and notion that individuals from my region and province were not that bright and, therefore, were certainly less intelligent than the rest of Mpugu's ethnic groups. In an effort to attempt to prove the assertion wrong, Professor Onkere, who rarely brags about his own brothers and sisters' scholarly accomplishments, pointed out that there were many highly qualified doctors within his own family—Dr. Randy, Dr. Dah, Dr. Opy, and Dr. Onkere himself—on top of his sisters holding master's and bachelor's degrees, as well as those holding teaching and nursing professional degrees. He went on, explaining that each of his sisters and brothers was an outstanding performer in their respective field, three of whom were actually teaching at the university level. He argued that people should normally be judged not on the content of their place of birth or ethnicity or religion or even on their race. Instead, he pointed out, as so well established by Dr. Martin Luther King Jr., individuals should be judged by the content of their character and on their merit. He went on, arguing that worldwide, in every continent, nationality, nation, race, people, tribe, and ethnicity, one can almost always find highly intelligent people, slightly less intelligent people, and highly nonintelligent people. He contended that it actually was wrong to be judgmental by putting individuals into boxes. He went on, further explaining that the so-called racial theories advocating the superiority of one race on another, in America for example, during the fifties and sixties between whites and blacks, resulted in giving the first a false sense of superiority, while the latter felt a false sense of inferiority, paraphrasing Dr. Martin Luther King Jr. of course. From another standpoint, Professor Onkere also explained to that group of students that not far from Mpugu, on the African continent, one ethnic group considered itself superior to another ethnic group, and it was at the basis of literally the extermination of one ethnic group by another during one hundred days. The genocide he was alluding to occurred in the nineties.

Once back to his place that day, he went to his sister Olivia this time, to talk about what had transpired at the university and the arguments made on how that kind of preconceived notion should not be part of Mpugu's culture.

He reminded his sister what his arguments were. Later on that day, the discussion was brought to Professor Spencer's attention to get his opinion on the matter as well.

He basically sided with his colleague. While in America, for example, the race question is still a sensitive issue. In most African countries, the question of ethnicity or ethnic group, part of the social construct, remains a very sensitive issue. As such, it has been at the basis of politically motivated genocides and civil wars in some parts of Africa.

Reflecting on the discussion he had with his students, and especially the fact that there were now many university professors from Haute-Savana, Professor Onkere hoped it reinforced what he had been teaching. For those students, seeing Professor Onkere and, I might add, Professor Spencer, who was also from Akaga City, helped them understand that they could potentially do and accomplish anything they put their minds to. Furthermore, he also hoped they realized that nothing was impossible for whoever has the will and the determination, no matter the obstacles. That, of course, had been Professor Onkere's life, personal experiences, and story.

As for the university year, once again, it went well. From time to time, Professor Onkere would ask students to evaluate him and express how they felt about his teachings by suggesting what areas needed to be improved. He then would take into consideration all the suggestions in an attempt to get better and improve his way of teaching. At the end of that second year, grades, as requested by students, were calculated during an open session attended by the majority of them. After, he said goodbye to all of them, hoping to see them the following academic year.

Meanwhile, he was still working as an adviser in charge of international relations, devoting all his summer to dealing with issues related to international diplomacy. In his capacity as an adviser, he sat on more than three boards of directors, thereby representing his immediate boss.

Adviser Onkere's immediate boss was a highly competent man who had what it took to get a job well done. Adviser Onkere appreciated working with him. He had integrity and was fully aware of the notion of accountability that was of the greatest importance to the protagonist, who had with his boss a cordially civilized, professional relationship, based on mutual respect and understanding. Still, in his capacity as an adviser, the protagonist had two assistants. One was his personal assistant. He also had cabinet members. For some reasons irrelevant to this story, however, he worked particularly closely with some of them. All of them were dynamic young people he got on well with. He appreciated working with all of them, as they reciprocated having him as their boss.

While the academic year was still out, Professor Onkere traveled back to America to spend some quality time with his wife and children. The latter had been attending school in America. His children were all grown-up. Professor Onkere was beaming with joy upon seeing his kids and wife, who came to welcome him at the airport. The kids were all joyfully paying attention to his every move and word. In short, it felt good to see everybody again.

SUMMER BREAK

The summer break lasted for about two weeks, during which he reconnected the best possible way with his wife and kids, while trying to accomplish as much as he could with them before returning to Africa, where the academic year was going to resume. While in America, he, his kids, and his wife would go hang out at one of the biggest commercial spots where some luxury stores are located. The mall, it's called, is also a place where young ladies and gentlemen hang out while shopping.

In the mall, one would find lots of stores. There, individuals could also find jewelry stores, food courts, relaxing spots, bookstores, or even playgrounds for kids to enjoy themselves. Onkere would take his kids and wife there to do some clothing shopping and eat at some fancy restaurants. After being in America for some weeks, the protagonist returned to Bonneville, Africa, to resume his professional activities, starting with academia.

BONNEVILLE UNIVERSITY: YEAR 3

The academic year that started was going to be his last. Indeed, he had already been approached with a potential position overseas. Yet by the time school resumed, he did not know when the appointment would be made, let alone where he was likely going to be sent to and whether or not he would accept the offer. It was a wait-and-see kind of moment. Considering all the uncertainties that could come with the position, Professor Onkere did not discuss the issue right away with his wife. He kept it sort of a secret until things were clear enough for him to have a conversation with his wife.

While waiting for the new appointment, he was assigned three sophomore classes. He would teach Applied English,

Phonetics, and American Civilization. Basically, by the third year of him teaching at the university, he had been moved to only teach sophomore classes. Midway through the school year, he was finally appointed to America, as an adviser to the Great Organization in Washington, DC. To that appointment, there was nothing he could do but accept the offer. Consequently, the decision was made that at the end of the school year, he would actually return to the United States. Upon receiving the news, he felt compelled to share it right away with his students.

Many of them were saddened by it. Others had mixed feelings. A few were genuinely delighted for him. Yet, at the same time, the majority felt they would lose a highly engaged and determined professor who had been not only like a role model to many but also a sort of motivational speaker for them. Nevertheless, he kept teaching at the university till the end of the school year, while attending his other job as an adviser.

At this point, I feel the necessity to indicate that Professor Onkere taught for some academic years at the university, almost for free. By the time he started his appointment as an adviser in charge of international relations, a national law had been signed forbidding public servants like him to have two combined sources of income from the government. The law further stipulated that public servants had to pick one source of income from the different positions entitling them to be paid. In that regard, Professor Onkere picked his advisory-related income. In most cases, once the source of income was picked, some public servants possessing more than two positions, knowing they would not be paid anymore, gave up working for the other position. As for

Professor Onkere, regardless of this new law, his passion for teaching and sharing his knowledge with his little sisters and brothers was so intensely ridiculous that nothing could derail him from teaching.

He kept teaching but was not being paid for what he was doing. Remarkably enough, for the duration of those years, he never missed any of his classes. He was never late either. During his tenure, he always showed up fifteen or even thirty minutes ahead of time. He would take that time to talk with his students in order to always try to get to know them better.

From getting to know some of his students, he understood that they came from different backgrounds and were dealing with different personal issues at home. While some came from very decent families, some others came from modest and low-income working families.

Students belonging to this last category were struggling to get to the university. Sometimes, some of them would be short of money. To those students, I would personally help them out by offering bus money because I genuinely understood where they came from. I would make it clear to those students that I was not doing this out of pity. I would explain to them that while growing up, I myself would walk miles on foot, during long, exhausting hours, to get to school when I was in primary and later on in high school. I would furthermore explain that I needed to help them out with bus money so that tomorrow, in the future, they could pass the humanitarian baton to the next generation. I believe, and still do, that Professor Onkere's outstanding humanity and incredibly positive compassion, inherited from both of his parents, contributed to some of his students literally crying their hearts out upon hearing that he was returning to America.

A week before school was out, Professor Onkere was still encouraging his students to keep working hard and not lose hope. To the ones who had already picked him to be their master thesis supervisor, he did apologize and asked them to keep in touch so that wherever he was, he could still help them in some way. I can assure you that he kept his word. Once the school year was over, Professor Onkere was ready to travel back to the United States of America. In the meantime, because he needed to boost his credentials in diplomacy, given that he had been appointed to the Great Organization, one of the highest levels of international diplomacy to represent his country, it was highly important for him to undergo some training in that field. More specifically, the focus was put on what is referred to as multilateral diplomacy as opposed to bilateral diplomacy. He underwent a four-month intensified training at the Department of International Relations.

He was placed under the leadership of a seasoned diplomat whose longstanding carrier was carried out mostly in the Great Organization Headquarters in Washington, DC. He could not wish for better. As the fast learner he is, Adviser Onkere acquired fundamental concepts and positions taken by his country on issues debated in the Great Organization Headquarters. Upon completing his training, he was more than ready to fly to Washington, DC, via Boston.

CHAPTER 10

The Great Organization

The achievements of an organization are the results
of the combined effort of each individual.
—Vince Lombardi

THE BOSTON TRIP

Marital and fatherhood obligations made Adviser Onkere
travel to Boston first, on his way to Washington, DC. His
wife and children had been living there by themselves since
returning to America. The trip to Boston was also of the
greatest importance, given that his wife and children had
been asking for him. He missed them and needed, therefore,
to be by their side. Everybody was delighted to have him
back. He would spend two weeks with his family before
flying to DC, where he had been appointed.

Two weeks after he got to Boston, he then traveled
to Washington, DC, to fill out administrative documents
relative to his new appointment. Once in DC, he went
straight to the office to meet with his new boss, who was

expecting him. Upon discussing his appointment with the latter, it was determined that he would start his new job the next day. In the meantime, he had to spend about one week at a hotel located somewhere downtown.

In order to help him find a decent residence, his wife and youngest son, Owny, the couple's cheerful baby, traveled with him to Washington, DC, to look for what would be their house and eventually the neighborhood they would reside in. Considering that the couple had children, it was determined that Adviser Onkere and his family would not reside in Washington, DC. Instead, they would find a residence in Maryland, one of the neighboring states, where there seemed to be more tranquility and fewer attractions. The calmness and quietness of that state, it was argued, would give their kids the opportunity to be more focused on school and not get distracted by the many attractions that could be found in Washington, DC. Both Adviser Onkere and his wife agreed on that proposal. Eventually, they ended up getting a nice residence in Maryland.

The residence was a Victorian splendor built near a local river. A pure Maryland architectural jewel, the house was built around the 1870s. It had tall windows and a ten-foot ceiling with intricate plaster moldings. Its pocket doors together with its triple bay window as well as its Italianate exterior were features characterizing its style. The house had three levels connected by old Victorian stairs. It had six bedrooms and two full bathrooms on the second and third floors. Appliances included a dishwasher, dryer, range, oven, refrigerator, and washer. The floor size was 2,894 square feet. Its floor was made of carpet, hardwood, laminate, and tile. The house had ceiling fans and an old Victorian fireplace that still works up to this day. The residence was simply expensively gorgeous, to the satisfaction of Mrs. Onkere Smith, who had made sure that it was downtown in walking distance from shops, restaurants, movie theaters, gyms, and the like.

Basically, Adviser Onkere and his family would live there, while he commuted to Washington, DC, where the Great Organization Headquarters was located, as was his office on First Avenue, not far from the organization. Prior to starting his appointment, however, he went back to Boston to get some furniture and materials for the new residence. His wife had insisted that some unused furniture from their private residence be taken to the new place together with kids' stuff and her own things. Once back in Boston, Adviser Onkere spent just two days, during which a moving truck was rented and all the furniture that was going to be taken to Maryland was loaded in. That night, the decision was also made to hit the road early in the morning. The following morning, as scheduled, the adviser got the family van packed with the kids, the two pets, Bisous and Penny, and some additional material, while his wife and their older daughter got the rented moving truck. The entire family drove for about seven hours from Boston to Maryland via I-95 S. Considering that the kids were all complaining about literally everything, after driving for about two hours, a decision was quickly made over the phone from husband to wife to stop at some restaurant and have lunch. After, they continued their driving. They got to their final destination late that day and went straight to bed around seven.

Once the adviser started his appointment, his boss suggested that he be in charge of special questions. This meant that he would be in charge of bilateralism while working in the Great Organization. All the advisers, as well as his boss, would also be working in close contact with this international organization. Still, in his capacity as an adviser, Onkere was assigned to the Third Committee of the Great Organization, where he would be working in close contact with one of his colleagues named Jay-Jay, whom he had actually known while socializing with Fefe back in Africa. Jay-Jay, as a matter of fact, was Fefe's roommate back at Bonneville University. By now, he had been working at the Great Organization for some years and was a brilliant and seasoned diplomat. His insights would be helpful to Onkere. Furthermore, it was decided that the latter would have his office next to that of a seasoned diplomat by the name of Bello. He was in charge of one of the committees.

At this point, I feel the necessity to briefly recall not only some of the main reasons why the Great Organization came into being but also how it works.

THE GREAT ORGANIZATION

The Great Organization is an international organization established on June 6, 1970, with the objective of preventing wars worldwide. The majority of the world's countries are part of this organization. Adviser Onkere's own country, Mpugu, is part of it. As of now, there are about two hundred member states. Lingala, English, and French are the only three official languages used at the Great Organization. In 1970, the organization drafted its charter in Mpugu, Africa.

Basically, it lays out the principles needed to be observed by the international community in order to avoid and prevent wars. Naturally, peace prevention and peacekeeping are crucial components of its mission. The Great Organization has seven main bodies or entities, among which are the General Meeting, the Security House, the Social Council, the Secretariat, the Economic Council, the Court of Justice, and the Trusteeship Council. The Security House, the entity whose main role is to maintain world peace and security, has eight permanent members. The rest of the countries have a rotated nonpermanent membership that allows them to sit in on the Council House from time to time. Additionally, to these seven main entities, the Great Organization has six main committees: the First Committee, which deals with all questions relative to disarmament and international security; the Second Committee, which discusses economic and financial questions.

The Third Committee, which Adviser Onkere was assigned to, examines social, humanitarian, and cultural issues. The Fourth Committee analyzes questions relative to special politics and decolonization. The Fifth Committee works on administrative and budgetary matters. And last but not least, the Sixth Committee examines all the legal questions. Advisers are assigned to these respective committees in accordance with their backgrounds.

Even so, Adviser Onkere was assigned, as already mentioned, to the Third Committee, which most specifically examines questions relative to social development, crime, drugs, advancement of women, or rights of children. This committee also examines questions of human rights, racism, and self-determination.

Given that countries are primarily part of the Great Organization to make sure their multiform interests are protected, sometimes being part of a group gives a country more strength and power to reach that goal. This is why Adviser Onkere's country is part of the African Club amongst the other Great Organization's groups represented within the organization.

Less than six months into his capacity as an adviser, Onkere had to go through his first General Meeting session experience. As it turned out, it was the Fifty-Sixth General Meeting. During those high-level sessions, heads of member states gather in Washington, DC, at the Great Organization Headquarters. This means that there are intensely political and diplomatic activities going on during this period of time. For new members of any representation, there is immeasurable pressure put on them as well as on their immediate bosses. As for Adviser Onkere, who just got appointed, he was not stressed out at all. He always remains cool under pressure and tends to keep a relaxed and laid-back kind of attitude, which his wife adores.

As it turned out, during that November, the representation of Mpugu to the Great Organization took over the chairmanship of the African Club. Consequently, all the advisers from that representation would normally be chairing the committees mentioned earlier. Ultimately, Adviser Onkere was assigned to chair the Third Committee of the African Club experts to the Great Organization. In the meantime, ongoing debates went on at the Great Organization Headquarters. Heads of states had to take the floor to make statements about issues crucially important to their respective countries. In that perspective, Ngantsie, Mpugu's head of state, made an excellently brilliant case about issues relevant to his country. At the end of his passionate advocacy for his country, Ngantsie received an amazingly well-deserved standing ovation.

While working at the representation of Mpugu to the Great Organization, Adviser Onkere was part of a team of negotiators who worked on a resolution involving sexual harassment instrumentally initiated by his country.

Coming out of those negotiations, he understood that in order to get the job done at the Great Organization, diplomats had to be open-minded and flexible. They must also be excellent negotiators ready to compromise and strike deals. Ultimately, consensus is one of the keywords diplomats must constantly have in mind whenever they negotiate.

THE ENGLISH LANGUAGE RELEVANCY

One of the key elements when it comes to working at the Great Organization is how well any diplomat working on behalf of their country can fluently speak and impeccably understand the English language. In this particular regard, Adviser Onkere had proven on numerous occasions that he could not only fluently speak English, but he also could understand it. Even though Lingala and French are the other official languages to be considered while working at the Great Organization, delegates from French-speaking countries tend to unwillingly be forced to speak English during negotiations, plenary sessions, or official meetings. Many factors, irrelevant to this story, could easily be explained. One of them is the fact that original texts distributed within the Great Organization Headquarters are primarily written in English. This language, being one of the most spoken internationally, makes it a kind of temptation for everyone wanting to speak it.

THE NATIONAL CAPACITY

Midway through the Fifty-Sixth General Meeting, delegations were to make statements on a national capacity about issues raised by the secretariat that had an impact domestically or nationally. In that regard, Adviser Onkere eagerly felt compelled to make a statement on Issue 70 (a, b) within the Third Committee he was assigned to. Issue 70 (a, b) is relative to sexual harassment and how his country positions itself on this issue. To do so, a statement draft had to be made and then presented during a cabinet meeting to the rest of his colleagues for input, discussion, and ultimately debate.

During the discussions that ensued, instead of making positive criticism and constructive proposals, Adviser Onkere felt that some of his colleagues were being unprofessional and harshly criticizing the stylistic way he had tackled the issue at hand, by not incorporating the Great Organization's way of presenting official statements.

He waited for another cabinet meeting involving, this time, their boss to express concerns about the way forward. During that meeting, he argued how stylistic differences that might have existed—pointed out by some colleagues— were due to his education background. Yet he expressed the willingness to apply the Great Organization's way of presenting official documents and statements. However, he made it clear that there was no reason whatsoever to be so diplomatically unprofessional.

Prior to heading to Maryland, following his appointment, he actually had already anticipated that such misunderstandings could likely occur. He had also long ago figured out that he did have what it took to efficiently accomplish the job for which he had been appointed to the Great Organization. Indeed, he believed that the governmental authorities who had appointed him went through his résumé, where his credentials are clearly established. He was fluent in English and knew a lot about America, its culture, and its politics—tools needed at the Great Organization, especially considering the fact that English-speaking superpowers set, most of the time, the organization's agenda. In this particular regard, it seemed important for diplomats assigned to the organization to be aware of the American political system as it was specifically related to the party's ideology. Being aware of American political ideologies, for example, could allow diplomats assigned to the organization to understand how American presidents from either party stood on American domestic issues. And, on the other hand, how the party's ideology could impact the president's foreign policy, which, for the most part, could be reinforced through the United States' representation to the organization. Adviser Onkere had a deep understanding and grasp of the American political system together with its institutions, on top of his understanding of the world order as well as international diplomacy.

His résumé, furthermore, should establish that he had interacted with world scholars, preachers, politicians, civil rights leaders, and students while teaching both French and English at different American, European, and African top universities, that he had had a training at the Department of International Relations back home, and so on and so forth. All things considered, it seems to me that it could be a diplomatic mistake for anyone to believe that a person with such a background could not be an asset for any representation to the Great Organization. Among the advisers who clearly got his point was Miss Land, who expressed her embarrassment with the entire ordeal he went through.

After the adviser willingly set the record straight, the head of the representation ironed out any misunderstanding that transpired during the previous meeting. Following that day, Adviser Onkere came to find out that some of his colleagues still made some criticisms but in a very professional manner, which he greatly appreciated. The next week following the last cabinet meeting, Adviser Onkere went to the Great Organization Headquarters and made an outstanding statement on behalf of his country on the issue of harassment.

THE AFRICAN CLUB CHAIRMANSHIP

When Mpugu took over the African Club chairmanship, Adviser Onkere's immediate boss, a pragmatically trained lawyer, efficiently chaired the club at its highest level. Onkere was assigned to chair the African Club experts of the Third Committee, where all the debates and discussions were carried out solely in English, even though French-speaking countries are part of the club. But, for reasons, some of which have already been explained, sessions were carried out in English.

As such, the chairperson—regardless of his or her official language—is expected to express himself or herself only in English. The English language becomes therefore imperative, the key needed to unlock doors allowing navigation through the labyrinth that happens to be the Great Organization.

Chairing the African Club was the ideal moment to show what Adviser Onkere was capable of. Given the feedback received from his colleagues from other countries, he did an excellent job. First, being a Francophone and thus speaking French, the diplomat he had become surprised more than one with the way he conducted the debates in English. He not only impressed French-speaking colleagues, but he, above all, amazed English-speaking ones.

He mastered extraordinarily well the back and forth between the various interests representing the different African countries who were part of the club.

The diplomat exhibited an unusual easiness during the debates, indicative of how he appropriately mastered the art of public speaking, together with that of chairing a club composed of seasoned diplomats knowing that he was just less than six months into exercising his new position. More specifically, the diplomat demonstrated an incredible capacity and amazing open-mindedness to comprehend issues being discussed during the debates. In his capacity as chairperson of the African Club, Adviser Onkere held more than fifteen meetings within three weeks.

THE COMMUTE

During the days the meetings were held, he had to get up around five in the morning and get out of the residence around six thirty. The rationale behind him waking up early had to do with him commuting from Maryland to

Washington, DC. On ordinary days, buses would take one hour and thirty minutes to get from Maryland to his final destination. And because of this, he had to get up early. Also, whenever the traffic was jammed, the commute could take almost two hours. To avoid being caught in such a case, the best thing for the diplomat to do was to make sure he got off the road before nine in the morning when traffic was still slow.

By that time, all the express buses taking only highway routes were already gone. In such a case, the only choice for the diplomat was to take local buses that made stops almost every other five minutes. With that kind of motion, the diplomat would get to meetings late.

This is why he had to wake up early in the morning, to avoid being caught up in traffic jams or any of the other mentioned eventualities. Waking up early over a month was hard on him. During the commute, he listened to music on his device or read a book. Listening to music would either help in waking him up or keep him from falling asleep. During the rides, the musically inclined diplomat would listen to some of his favorite singers, such as Dolly Parton, Luther Vandross, Norah Jones, Elton John, John Legend, and Passenger, to name a few. More specifically, he would listen to Luther Vandross's "Once We're Lovers," Elton John's "Daniel," John Legend's "All of Me," Norah Jones's "The Nearness of You," Dolly Parton's "Backwoods Barbie," Passenger's "Somebody's Love," "Let Her Go," and "Riding to New York." These were some touching and moving songs that would keep him from falling asleep. On some other occasions, he would read some of the books making headlines or unfinished ones whose reading was stopped at some point. The majority of those books examined American political and race issues. From the period that the Fifty-Sixth Great Organization General Meeting started, while commuting five days out of seven from Maryland to Washington, DC, midway through January of the following year, he had read the following books: Carol Anderson's *White Rage: The Unspoken Truth of Our Racial Divide* (2016); James Baldwin's *The Evidence of Things Not Seen* (1995); Joseph Barndt's *Understanding and Dismantling Racism: The Twenty-First Century Challenge to White America* (2007); Edward Klein's *The Amateur: Barack Obama in the White House* (2012); Judith A. Best's *The Choice of the People? Debating the Electoral College* (1996); and George C. Edward III's *Why the Electoral College Is Bad for America?* (2004).

Reading these books helped him cope with any situation going on at the Great Organization Headquarters and more specifically among the African Club experts.

Some days, Adviser Onkere had to convene and chair three to four meetings. Most of the time, debates were very tough among the parties involved, to a degree that during such moments, exceptional leadership abilities were required from the chairperson; otherwise, the meetings could have been derailed, and ultimately, the credibility of the chairperson and his ability to manage the club could have been questioned. Fortunately for Adviser Onkere, things went well during his chairmanship, even though at some moments he had to raise his voice and step up to the plate to bring order among the representatives of the African member states of the Great Organization. Some other times, debates went well, and everyone got along with the rest of the representatives of member states. It was during his chairmanship that Adviser Onkere understood what such words as loyalty, compromise, consensus, and deal meant, even though he had already gone through steps involved in a negotiation process.

Retrospectively, I can argue that one of the reasons Adviser Onkere successfully chaired the African Club has to do with him being first and foremost a university assistant professor. As such, he was used to be in front of people, while demonstrating an easiness as well as an exceptional ability in expressing himself. Many of the meetings that were held ultimately resulted in the club coming out with real proposals and contributions that were made known to all the Great Organization member states. Indeed, during plenary sessions, on behalf of the African countries, Adviser Onkere, in his capacity as the chairperson of the African Club members, had the great honor and privilege to take the floor more than five times in front of all of the Great Organization's members, representing two hundred states. Out of those five times, the diplomat made three statements, all of which were singularly more than well performed in the English language.

The statements were written by the advisers who were following the discussions during the negotiations on behalf of the African Club with its counterparts. However, once the drafts were presented to the club, they became, in the end, a collaborative effort whose inputs were agreed upon by all the African members under the supervision of the club's coordinator. Still, once final drafts were brought to his attention, the chairperson naturally proofread and punctuated them accordingly to his liking. He also added elements he deemed missing while fixing them as he saw fit. The easiness, the body language, gestures, intonation rising and falling, and the eye contact the diplomat maintained throughout his performances were all indicative of how excellent a communicator he was. In fact, he had taught communication classes. As such, he perfectly knew what had to be done during a speech delivery, even though the clock was set to go off past five minutes, the time allocated to speakers making statements on behalf of a regional group such as the African Club. As for the statements he so eloquently made, I remember that the first one was made on the resolution entitled "Promotion and Protection of the Rights of the Disabled." Whereas, the second statement was made on the resolution entitled "Social Development." As for the third, it was about women's empowerment.

There was the young boy from Akaga City, Adviser Onkere, the father, husband, professor, and diplomat, almost two decades after he first came across the English language, making statements in that same language at the Great Organization, one of the highest international diplomatic stages, on behalf of the African Club members and their respective countries. Those moments were of paramount importance, and diplomats representing two hundred countries were religiously and carefully listening to the African case being outstandingly made by our main protagonist, who was also loyally representing his own beloved country, Mpugu. It was during those crucial, determining, and pinnacle moments of his career as a diplomat that he realized, as a French-speaking person, the remarkable role as well as the exceptional importance of his mastering the English language.

PLENARY SESSION ANALYSIS

After the plenary sessions, some of his African colleagues, most likely from not only French but also English-speaking countries, approached him. They expressed their gratitude to him for such brilliant performances. Some of the comments made were that he impressed more than just one of his colleagues. For the most part, they were amazed by the way the diplomat sounded and the ease with which he made the case on behalf of the African countries.

The other stories told were that diplomats at the Great Organization Headquarters were accustomed to hearing diplomats from the club speak English with a certain distinctive diction. Most of the time, featured speakers were expected to be from English-speaking countries because, obviously, English happened to be their official language. This meant that diplomats from French-speaking countries, even though they might speak English, were rarely sent out to perform in English during plenary sessions. If they did, they would do so in French. The surprise was, therefore, remarkably reinforced with Adviser Onkere being from a French-speaking country while sounding, at the same time, highly confident and excellent while performing. While the protagonist was making the case on behalf of African countries, one of his colleagues was home watching plenary sessions online. She, later on, would confess to Adviser Onkere that while the latter was making his case, she kept wondering who he was and which African, English-speaking country he came from. She was so impressed by what she was watching online that she could not believe the protagonist was actually from a French-speaking country, simply because she had never heard, up to that day, any French-speaking diplomat from the Third Committee of the African Club expressing himself the way the protagonist did.

Adviser Onkere's performances went so smoothly, to the degree that his colleague who unconsciously was expecting an unexpected occurrence during the diplomat's deliveries was so relieved because, according to her, nothing bad happened. For example, had he gone over the five minutes allocated for the type of statements he made, his microphone could have been shut off, thus constituting a serious embarrassment not only to the African Club but also to the whole continent. She genuinely expressed how good she felt about his performances and suggested that, in her humble opinion, what she watched during those sessions, other diplomats and representatives of other nations might have seen it as well. That they too might have been impressed with Adviser Onkere's performances. Many colleagues from the African Club also congratulated the protagonist. A dear colleague and friend of his, a remarkably outstanding diplomat he had become close to during his chairmanship, confessed to him how amazingly impressed he was and how he professionally led the club. His colleague also revealed how incredible and exceptional all three of his performances were during plenary sessions. He told Adviser Onkere, long after the latter's chairmanship was done, how mutual colleagues of theirs kept asking after him during ordinary sessions occurring at the Great Organization Headquarters among experts of the African Club. This seemed to be accurate because whenever Onkere came across any African colleague from the club, they would always end up asking him where he had been.

Also, Evry, one of his former students who came to visit him at the Great Organization almost fifteen years after they had first met, congratulated him upon viewing the videos relative to his performances.

Unfortunately, given that a coin always has two faces, not everyone was satisfied or appreciated the excellent performances made by Adviser Onkere during his chairmanship, let alone while making cases on behalf of the African Club during plenary sessions. I believe that some among the African Club members became dissatisfied with him being praised pretty much by everyone, almost all the time. The dissatisfaction, however, was more implied through words coming out during small talks than through any gesture or behavior. After all, are we not diplomats?

CHAIRMANSHIP ENDS

At the end of his tenure as chairperson of the African Club, Adviser Onkere felt compelled to send an email out to all his African colleagues who graciously had congratulated him, while recognizing his brilliance and his managerial and exceptional leadership skills demonstrated throughout the meetings, the debates, and ultimately during the plenary sessions. In that same vein, I, too, sent out an email to my colleagues, in which I essentially informed them of the end of Mpugu's chairmanship for the month of November. Therefore, I really felt compelled to thank all my colleagues for their extraordinary collaboration. It seemed appropriate for me to say that all of them were incredible, open-minded hard workers and outstanding diplomats. I had come to enjoy working with each and every one of them. I explained to them that, ultimately, their commitment and hard work made it possible, during the plenary, for all our resolutions to be adopted either by consensus or by vote. As Africans, I argued, we all understood that no one but ourselves would give us anything to help develop our continent. It seemed, therefore, up to all of us African diplomats assigned to the Great Organization to keep doing our part by having resolutions adopted. Development, I argued, if we wanted it for our continent, we, African diplomats assigned to the Great Organization needed more work, consistency, punctuality, unity, love, understanding, mutual respect, open-mindedness, and, of course, strong diplomacy to accomplish this goal one bright day. Whatever positive change we so desire for Africa, I contended, if we were serious about it, we African diplomats assigned to the Great Organization had to fight for it. For, as someone had so eloquently pointed out, change does not roll in on the wheels of inevitability but comes through continuous struggle. Therefore, we African diplomats assigned to the Great Organization must straighten our backs and work for it because a man can't ride us unless our backs are bent; I quoted, of course, Dr. King. Economic justice for Africa, I contended, if we wanted it, brothers and sisters, ladies and gentlemen, we must fight for it in the Great Organization. And for that, we needed, once again, more cooperation, more work, and more collaboration among ourselves first before taking the diplomatic fight to others. We must be more dedicated to what we, African diplomats, have been sent here to do. Dr. Martin Luther King Jr., one of my brothers from another mother, used to say that human progress is neither automatic nor inevitable and that every step toward the goal of justice requires sacrifice, suffering, and struggle, the tireless exertions and passionate concern of dedicated individuals—I wrote. In this spirit, I remained very hopeful and strongly confident that we African diplomats assigned to the Great Organization can do our part and get the ball of economic justice rolling—I kept writing. Collaborating with all of you for about four weeks allowed me to come across very intelligent, bright ladies and gentlemen, experienced diplomats who knew the issues being discussed. I can only encourage all of us to keep working harder toward understanding not only the issues being discussed and talked about at the headquarters but also strategies and techniques used to get things done in the Great Organization. Your guidance and input helped me a great deal. I ended up concluding my email on that note.

In the final analysis, this is a tale that each and every one of us should tell, narrate, and share. Each of us, I strongly believe, has a story that can be told, and this was Onkere's. It all started with an unexpected encounter that developed into a dream and ultimately materialized through resilience and determination.

Epilogue

This story remains unfinished business, as Onkere's wife would remind him, given that he still has a long way to go before closing chapters on his experiences as related both to the English language and American culture. As of now, I do not know and cannot predict when the next chapter about his love story with the English language is going to be narrated. All I know with certainty is that, at the end of the day, after more than two decades from the time of his first encounter with the English language, he is still working toward improving his way of sounding and expressing himself, while looking for new opportunities to acquire new vocabulary, idioms, and expressions. It is fair and safe, however, to say that he is not only an accomplished international scholar who acquired more than just the basic necessities for him to speak or teach English, communication, and American studies to university students across three continents—Europe, America, and Africa. He is also a seasoned diplomat who excellently represented not only his beloved country, Mpugu, but also the entire African continent during ordinary as well as plenary sessions, using the English language at one of the highest levels of international diplomacy—the Great Organization located in Washington, DC. Ultimately, this story was shared so as to make the point about the value of resilience as well as hard work in overcoming hardships. It's also a testimony that brilliance and success are neither ethnic group-based nor country of origin-related, and that determination always pays off.

Lightning Source UK Ltd.
Milton Keynes UK
UKHW010846260719
346818UK00001B/5/P

9 781532 076053